THE 8 SECRETS TO INTENTIONALLY CHANGE YOUR FORTUNE

1. Commit to Be a VLP—Very Lucky Person

2. Release Your Personal Barriers to Good Fortune

3. Transform Shame into a Magnet for Abundance

4. Have Luck-Worthy Goals

5. Take Bold Action Consistently

6. Find Your Lucky Tribe

7. Learn to Be at the Right Place at the Right Time

8. Practice Radical Gratitude and Appreciation

Advance Praise for *Conscious Luck*

"If being luckier appeals to you, you've got to read this book! Luck isn't as random as you might think. The secrets in *Conscious Luck* will accelerate your journey from where you are to where you want to be."
—Jack Canfield, coauthor of the #1 *New York Times* bestselling Chicken Soup for the Soul series and *The Success Principles™: How to Get from Where You Are to Where You Want to Be*

"*Conscious Luck* takes everything you know about luck . . . and turns it on its head! This is an engaging, mind-blowing, and ultimately practical guide to creating more luck in your life. I highly recommend it!"
—Marci Shimoff, #1 *New York Times* bestselling author of *Happy for No Reason* and *Chicken Soup for the Woman's Soul*

"*Conscious Luck* is as unique as it is powerful. It approaches luck from many different angles—somatically, psychologically, spiritually, and behaviorally—and uses true, inspiring stories to illustrate the principles."
—John Gray, #1 *New York Times* bestselling author of *Men Are from Mars, Women Are from Venus*

"*Conscious Luck* presents an entirely new paradigm about luck—instead of passively waiting and hoping for luck to find you, these two brilliant authors show you how to create good luck by changing your core beliefs about luck and incorporating easy, simple practices into your daily life. A lucky life is waiting for you."
—Arielle Ford, author of *The Soulmate Secret*

"Gay Hendricks and Carol Kline are the luck mentors everyone needs! Their new book, *Conscious Luck,* is a winning combination of inspiring true stories and simple, practical steps designed to create more luck in life. Give yourself the gift of good fortune."
—Katherine Woodward Thomas, *New York Times* bestselling author of *Calling in "The One"*

"Your life is about to become supercharged with positive transformation abilities as you read, absorb, and use the secrets in *Conscious Luck*!"
—Mark Victor Hansen, author of titles in the Chicken Soup for the Soul series, *One Minute Millionaire,* and *Ask! The Bridge from Your Dreams to Your Destiny*

"I'm a firm believer in the power of clarity and persistence to create success. Add the ability to create your own luck to the equation and watch your growth and happiness soar. *Conscious Luck* is a game-changer."

—Jeff Olson, bestselling author of *The Slight Edge: Turning Simple Disciplines into Massive Success and Happiness,* and the CEO and founder of Neora

"Luck isn't just a matter of chance! *Conscious Luck* provides a practical formula for cultivating good luck in your life intentionally. Your core beliefs and daily habits are the key."

—Dr. John Douillard, globally recognized leader in the fields of natural health, Ayurveda, and sports medicine, and the bestselling author of *The 3-Season Diet*

"*Conscious Luck* is a toolkit for writing your own happy ending."

—Debbie Macomber, #1 *New York Times* bestselling author

"This is your lucky day! Authors Gay Hendricks and Carol Kline will teach you how to lead a successful, abundant, harmonious life. Reading *Conscious Luck* provides you with the missing elements that attract luck to you—in all areas of your life."

—Peggy O'Neill, inclusion and empowerment strategist, and the author of *Walking Tall: Overcoming Inner Smallness No Matter What Size You Are*

"*Conscious Luck* demonstrates that by focusing on specific practices you can dramatically increase your good fortune. This should be required reading for anyone who wants to create the life they dream to live."

—Tina Seelig, Ph.D., professor at Stanford University, and author of *What I Wish I Knew When I Was 20* and *Creativity Rules*

"I fought my skeptical tendencies while reading this book, but when I started regularly scoring prime parking spots within days of doing the exercises, I became a believer! Take on 'luck creation' as a lifestyle and watch your life change!"

—Laura Berman Fortgang, author of *Now What? 90 Days to a New Life Direction*

"I know *Conscious Luck* will be an important contribution to the life of every person who reads it. Highly recommended!"

—Neale Donald Walsch, author of the Conversations with God series

Also by Gay Hendricks:

The Big Leap

Conscious Loving

Five Wishes

Conscious Living

The Corporate Mystic

At The Speed of Life

Learning to Love Yourself

Also by Carol Kline:

Chicken Soup for the Pet Lover's Soul
with Jack Canfield, Mark Victor Hansen, and Dr. Marty Becker

Chicken Soup for the Cat & Dog Lover's Soul
with Jack Canfield, Mark Victor Hansen, and Dr. Marty Becker

Chicken Soup for the Mother's Soul 2
with Jack Canfield, Mark Victor Hansen, and Marci Shimoff

Chicken Soup for the Dog Lover's Soul
with Jack Canfield, Mark Victor Hansen, Dr. Marty Becker, and Amy Shojai

Chicken Soup for the Cat Lover's Soul
with Jack Canfield, Mark Victor Hansen, Dr. Marty Becker, and Amy Shojai

You've GOT to Read this Book: 55 People Tell the Story of the Book That Changed Their Life
with Jack Canfield and Gay Hendricks

Happy for No Reason: 7 Steps for Being Happy from the Inside Out
with Marci Shimoff

Love for No Reason: 7 Steps to Creating a Life of Unconditional Love
with Marci Shimoff

CONSCIOUS LUCK

EIGHT SECRETS TO INTENTIONALLY CHANGE YOUR FORTUNE

GAY HENDRICKS
and CAROL KLINE

ST. MARTIN'S
ESSENTIALS
NEW YORK

Published in the United States by St. Martin's Essentials, an imprint of St. Martin's Publishing Group

www.stmartins.com

Design by Meryl Sussman Levavi

Photo of Gay Hendricks: Mikki Willis

Photo of Carol Kline: Charlie Wedel (5Dcreations)

Library of Congress Cataloging-in-Publication Data

Names: Hendricks, Gay, author. | Kline, Carol, 1957- author.
Title: Conscious luck : eight secrets to intentionally change your fortune / Gay Hendricks and Carol Kline.
Description: First edition. | New York : St. Martin's Essentials, [2020]
Identifiers: LCCN 2019054418 | ISBN 9781250622945 (hardcover) | ISBN 9781250622952 (ebook)
Subjects: LCSH: Success. | Fortune. | Attitude (Psychology)
Classification: LCC BF637.S8 H387 2020 | DDC 158.1—dc23
LC record available at https://lccn.loc.gov/2019054418

First Edition: May 2020

10 9 8 7 6 5 4 3 2 1

To Katie, for forty-plus years of living proof that I'm the luckiest man on earth

To my husband, Larry, my luckiest choice ever

CONTENTS

Part One

An Invitation to Transformation

Part Two

The Four Foundational Secrets: Making Core Shifts About Luck

Part Three

The Four Daily Living Secrets:
Luck-Changing Practices to Do Every Day

Part Four

Keeping It Going

Sell your cleverness.
Invest in wonder.

—Rumi

✤

Luck is what happens when preparation meets opportunity.

—Attributed to Seneca

PART ONE

An Invitation to Transformation

AUTHORS' NOTE

IMPORTANT: PLEASE READ

This book has an interesting backstory—a lucky one!

Gay: I wrote the first draft of this manuscript in 2012 and sent it to my friend, author and editor Carol Kline, for her feedback. Carol was enthusiastic about the book but said in her opinion it would require substantial editing and additional content before publication. I was just beginning to write detective fiction, which I thoroughly enjoyed, and decided to give that my full attention and put *Conscious Luck* on the shelf for a while. Years passed. Whenever I ran into Carol—we live in the same small town in Southern California—she would invariably ask what I was going to do with the *Conscious Luck* manuscript. My answer was always the same: nothing, at least for the foreseeable future. Then one day in March 2017, Carol and I met by chance in the local grocery store, had our typical exchange, and went our separate ways. Later that afternoon, Carol called me. . . .

✣

Carol: That manuscript haunted me. From the moment I read it, I loved the concept of Conscious Luck and the material Gay had written. I kept thinking of it and felt strongly that it should be made available to the world. But I was busy, Gay was busy, and it just didn't seem that this marvelous manuscript was going to be rescued from oblivion. Then, on that March day in 2017, after running into Gay at the market, a startling idea rose up from somewhere deep inside me: call Gay and offer to coauthor the rest of the book with him. *That's crazy,* I told myself. *If he wanted it published, he could do it himself.* But I figured the worst that could happen is that he would say no.

He didn't—and that's why you're holding this book right now. Gay and I both feel lucky, lucky, lucky, to have worked on *Conscious Luck* together, and we know reading it will make you lucky, too.

✤

Gay: The first half of the book (through chapter 3) is the edited and updated version of the original manuscript I wrote those many years ago. It's mostly in the first person in my voice. Chapters 4 through 8 are the product of my collaboration with Carol. These chapters are written in the "we" voice, and in addition to my stories, there are first-person stories from Carol and others. I love the varied perspectives and experiences Carol and those we interviewed brought to the *Conscious Luck* project and couldn't be more pleased with the results. Enjoy!

—*Gay Hendricks and Carol Kline*

July 2019

PREFACE

A Radical New Path

Luck, good or bad, is the invisible play of mind upon affairs, the effect of mental aptitudes and habits which are not in sight, but which work and bring forth their due issues.

—James Vila Blake, *Essays*

Life is about to change for you.

You're about to make a big shift in consciousness—as big as when you first learned how to speak and understand language. This shift will make many things possible for you that were out of your reach until now.

The word "radical" comes from the Latin word meaning "root" or "core." To make a radical change is to change something at the very core of your being. That level of change is what this book makes possible for you now.

It's likely that a crucial piece is missing from your approach to creating what you want in your life. It was missing for me, and it was missing for many of the people I've worked with. So if it's missing for you, you're not alone. Countless intelligent, hardworking people are missing out on a remarkable path to abundant wealth and harmonious living, simply because they haven't looked in the right place. I want you to look carefully into that right place with me: focus all your powers of attention on this for a little while and you'll have a treasure you can draw on for the rest of your life.

It took scientists a long time to figure out that the ocean tides rise and fall according to an invisible force a quarter million miles away. If you're like me, it probably took you a while to figure out a similar great mystery about your own life: *The visible results you experience are created by invisible forces within you.*

I glimpsed the power of this mystery principle a few times growing up, but it wasn't until I was in my twenties that I discovered how it actually worked and how to apply it to my own life.

William James, the father of American psychology, has been credited with saying, "The greatest discovery of my generation is that a human being can alter his life by altering his attitudes of mind."

Let's start by "altering our attitudes of mind" about what it takes to flourish mentally, emotionally, physically, and financially. Creating success in all areas of your life is partly about having good ideas and working diligently to implement those ideas. However, good ideas and persistence are often not enough to get you to your goals. Sometimes, in fact, they're not even the most important part of creating success. There's a crucial factor—one of those invisible forces at work—that's often overlooked, and it's my intention here to show you what it is and what you can do about it.

What is this crucial, overlooked factor? It's luck. That's right—L-U-C-K. Most of us probably don't even think about it, because we don't realize luck can be changed. We think luck comes from outside of us and is bestowed on us by chance—if you're lucky, you're lucky, and if you're not, you're not. We're wrong. Though there will always be a random component to luck—both good and bad—a great deal of your luck *can* be changed, and quickly, with a little conscious attention on your part.

In the same way that there are rules for improving your health—get enough sleep, eat well, stay hydrated, exercise regularly—there are specific guidelines for improving your luck. These guidelines, which we call the Conscious Luck Secrets, are laid out for you in the following pages, and if you follow them, you're going to get luckier. In fact, it's easier to become lucky than it is to work harder.

Another way to look at our ability to create luck comes from Dr. Tina Seelig, professor at Stanford University in the Department of Management Science and Engineering, who says that the key is "understanding that luck is rarely a lightning strike—isolated and dramatic—but a wind that blows constantly. . . . You need to build a sail—made up of tiny behaviors—to catch [the winds of luck]." More than a century earlier, Indian poet Rabindranath Tagore is attributed with saying much the same thing: "The winds of grace are always blowing, but it is you that must raise your sails."

In this book, my coauthor, Carol, and I will show you, in enough detail for you to master it for yourself, how to intentionally change your fortune.

If you're skeptical about this possibility, you're in good company. When I first awakened to these possibilities, I was skeptical, too, but I'm not anymore. One reason is that I've used the Conscious Luck Secrets we're about to share with you to create significant good luck for myself. More important, I've worked with thousands of people around the world—helping them implement strategies for creating success in every imaginable situation—and I've seen how learning these Secrets has changed the equation for them at a fundamental level. You'll read a variety of stories throughout the book that will help illustrate this dynamic.

However, no matter how many stories you read or hear, all that ultimately matters is that you change your own luck. That's what you and Carol and I are up to in this book. If that's *your* sincere desire, let's work together to create some genuine, observable miracles in your life.

The Conscious Luck Secrets

This book contains eight secrets that will allow you to change your luck consciously—specifically, to get good luck firmly established at the root of your being. You may not yet know that you can re-create yourself as a very lucky person, but in these pages, we'll give you precise techniques for doing just that.

The first four Secrets enable you to make shifts at the core of your being, creating a firm foundation for cultivating Conscious Luck. The second four Secrets are daily practices that build on that foundation, turning those core shifts into luck-enhancing habits.

The first Conscious Luck Secret requires that you make a sincere commitment to intentionally change your fortune and create abundance in your life.

Making your own commitment is essential. This gets you into the game as an equal partner, engaging fully with the powerful principles in the book. Without a commitment, you're sitting on the sidelines watching others play the game. In games like football it can be fun to sit in the bleachers and cheer others on. In luck creation, that's not where the big fun is. The big fun in this process is in playing full-out, with your gut and your heart in the game at all times.

Based on this commitment and new point of view, you'll use the second Conscious Luck Secret to reestablish the natural good luck you were born with. You, like everyone on earth, were born with a great capacity for good luck. Then, like all of us, you fell under the spell of your family's beliefs, feelings, and needs. Later, you likely fell under the spell of society's collective belief that luck is a fixed, external factor. With repeated exposure to the beliefs of family and society, you began to think the way *they* think, to believe what *they* believe, to act the way *they* act. This is only natural—no need to give yourself a hard time for falling under the spell of old programming.

All you need to do is acknowledge that your capacity to attract good luck is influenced by your old programming, wherever it came from. Once you do that, you're free to install new programming to reclaim your own natural good luck.

Restoring your natural gift of good luck opens the door to the third Conscious Luck Secret: learning how to turn any feelings of shame you have into an attractor-field for luck. Most of us have an inner sense of shame that was instilled in us when we were young. Shame is a powerful force field that influences what happens to you in your life. We all need to realize that this force field can be transformed and dedicated to a new purpose. By following the steps laid out in the third Conscious Luck Secret to make a subtle inner adjustment, you can feel shame disappear from your body as you put it to work attracting abundance and luck.

The fourth Conscious Luck Secret reveals how your goals influence your luck. Having goals that engage your whole heart and spirit and, when accomplished, serve both you and others gives luck good reasons to visit. In chapter 4, you'll learn how to set luck-worthy goals that attract support from others, lead to greater success—and are also a whole lot of fun to achieve.

With these core shifts in place, you're ready to learn the four Daily Living Secrets, which are *practices you do every day*—taking bold action, being vigilant about the influences you allow in your life, staying true to yourself and your inner guidance, and cultivating authentic gratitude and appreciation. These Daily Living Secrets are quite simple and work spectacularly well when you practice them diligently, day in and day out, so they eventually become habitual and self-perpetuating.

Progress Check

Let's pause and see where we are.

Does what you've read so far pique your curiosity? Does it inspire you even a little bit? Are you ready to make a serious commitment to change your luck? Be honest. If you answered "No" to any of these questions, you're probably not a good candidate for this book right now. That doesn't mean there's anything wrong with you or with our approach, it's just that they're not a good fit at the moment. Let's part for now as friends and wish each other well.

If you're still with us, you're on track to take the life-transforming step of changing your luck. It's a big one, so you may wish to clear your "mental" decks and take a few deep breaths as you prepare to dive in. And perhaps even arm yourself with a cup of tea or other nourishing reinforcements.

Ready? Here we go.

INTRODUCTION

How to Change Your Luck: My Story and Yours

Used to think that luck wuz luck and nuthin' else but luck—

It made no diff'rence how or when or where or why it struck;

But sev'ral years ago I changt my mind, an' now proclaim

That luck's a kind uv science—same as any other game.

—Eugene Field, "How Salty Win Out,"
from *The Poems of Eugene Field*

I'm one of the luckiest people I've ever known. It wasn't always that way, though. There was a time when my luck was not very good at all. Then I made a conscious choice to be lucky—the same choice I'll invite you to make shortly. From the moment I made that choice, my own life took a turn for the better and, for the most part, hasn't stopped turning for the better ever since. That's what I want you to experience.

If being the luckiest person you can be appeals to you, here is the first major concept to entertain:

> *The simplest way to create abundance on all levels is by changing your luck. The knowledge that you can change your luck consciously is one of the most valuable assets you have.*

Successful people are often uncommonly lucky. In the course of writing this book, I asked many people who are living abundant lives if they were lucky. Their answers ranged from "You bet!" to "Hell, yeah!" Not one of them said "No."

So, consider the radical notion that the easiest way to invite more wealth and harmony into your life is to get luckier. Even if you're already lucky, you can become much luckier with an intention to consciously create more good fortune. We'll use a specific process to accomplish the goal of making you luckier. I've refined the process with lots of people during the past forty years. It truly works wonders. You don't have to take my word for it, though. When you go through the process, you'll feel your luck change in your body and spirit at the same time. Then, you'll begin to see external results that confirm the power of those inner changes. You won't have any doubt about whether it works for you or not.

Being Lucky Is Not a Matter of Luck

If you're convinced that luck is always just a matter of luck, all I can say is "Good luck!" But . . . if you've got an open mind, you can work a real miracle in your life.

> Would you consider another way to look at luck?
> Would you entertain the idea that luck can be a matter of conscious choice?

If you'll consider that idea, you're on your way to big wins. I know that many people have used my techniques to change their luck at the casino or the card table, and that's fine with me. But what really interests me is something much bigger than anything you can win in a casino or card game. I'm interested in helping you change your luck in life itself—where the jackpots are love and money and genuine success.

It may seem hard to believe you could accomplish what I'm talking about. It's perfectly natural to feel that way. In fact, I prefer you to be at least somewhat doubtful of what I'm telling you until you have some real experience with it. For now, all I ask is that you consider that it just might possibly be true. Then, decide for yourself when you see the proof begin to pour in.

How I Found It Out

> *People who believe they have bad luck create bad luck. . . . Those who believe they are very fortunate, that the world is a generous place filled with trustworthy people, live in exactly that kind of world.*
>
> —Chris Prentiss, *The Alcoholism and Addiction Cure*

Some people may be born lucky, but I wasn't one of them. I grew up in a tiny house in a lower-middle-class neighborhood in Florida. My mother had a seven-year-old son and was pregnant with me when my father died suddenly at age thirty-two, leaving her with $300 and a Buick that wasn't paid for. The great blessing of my childhood was that my grandparents lived up the street. During the turmoil of the first few years of my life, while my mother was trying to get her feet back on the ground, I spent most of my time with my grandparents. There was a lot of love in my family, but very little money, with everybody pretty much living paycheck to paycheck.

One day something magical happened—an event that showed me how luck really worked. I've never forgotten that moment, and once I became a clinical psychologist, I drew on it often to help people with their problems. Here's what happened: When I was fourteen, I went to an afternoon movie with my friend Danny. For some reason the movie theater was holding a drawing before the show. We'd all been invited to write our names on the back of our ticket stub if we wanted a chance to win a new watch.

Moments before the winning ticket was drawn, Danny leaned over to me and said, "Watch this—I'm going to win!" Then the theater manager reached into the popcorn bucket that contained the several hundred names. *He looked at the ticket in his hand and called out Danny's name!* I was astounded. Later I asked my friend how he knew. He told me he was lucky. He told me that he won just about any time there was a lottery or something else that required luck. I asked him if he was born that way and he laughed.

"No," he said, "I noticed that some people are lucky, and some aren't, so I just changed my mind one day and decided to be lucky." Today we call that "mind-set," and according to positive psychology research, it's a huge determinant for luck. Studies have shown that people who consider themselves lucky are far more likely to experience good luck in their lives.

Danny added matter-of-factly, "It's a lot easier to change your mind and be lucky than it is to keep on being unlucky."

When I heard that, I thought: *If he can be lucky, I can be lucky, too.* Danny was a good kid, but he wasn't special or different. I realized that I too had the power to change my own mind so that I attracted luck.

Then I had a flash of insight: people in my family didn't think of themselves as lucky, so they weren't. They saw themselves as hardworking people who just got by, so that's what they did: they just got by. There was nothing wrong with being a hardworking person who got by, but I wanted more for my life. I'd been born one way—into a bad-luck situation, with my father dying and my mom going into a tailspin—but there was no law that said I couldn't reinvent myself. In my view, the universe didn't care one way or the other if I was lucky. It was just a fluke that circumstances had turned out the way they had with my parents. Even though bad luck and misfortune had been the prevailing atmosphere around me as I was growing up, there was no universal requirement that I had to maintain the attitude I'd been born into.

Walking home after the movie, I decided to reconceive myself as a lucky person. I just decided to be lucky—to be the guy who won the watch rather than the guy sitting next to the guy who won the watch. Before that moment, I was in a place where luck didn't visit. After that moment, I was where luck came to celebrate. I'd started a good-luck streak that continues to this day.

The Immediate Payoff

Now, listen to the payoff. The week after my epiphany in the movie theater I was browsing in the local magazine shop, killing some time until a Tarzan movie started at that same theater. The magazine shop owner, Ned, was a dedicated coin collector, and his shop had a section for collectors of rare coins. I had just taken up the hobby myself and was becoming enthralled by it. I noticed Ned talking to an elderly man over in the coin section but paid no further attention to them.

A little while later, I left the store to go to the movies. As I walked out the door, I saw an expensive-looking briefcase sitting on the sidewalk next to a parking meter. I looked up and down the street to see who might have left the briefcase, but nobody was in sight. I picked up the briefcase and went back into the magazine store. I asked Ned if he had any idea whose briefcase it was. Ned's eyes widened and he practically pounced on it. It turned out the briefcase belonged to the elderly man I'd seen in the shop just minutes before. Ned said the man was a famous coin dealer, and the briefcase contained coins he'd been discussing with Ned. When the man left the shop, he had apparently set the briefcase down while he put change into the parking meter. Then he'd absentmindedly walked off without it.

Ned ran outside and saw that the man's car was still parked, so he asked me to go around the corner to the local restaurant to see if the man had perhaps gone off to have lunch. My movie was about to start, though, so I begged off and headed to the theater.

Later, I learned that a huge drama had taken place while I was watching Tarzan, Jane, and Cheeta. The coin dealer was in the restaurant when he suddenly realized his briefcase was missing. He thought someone in the restaurant had stolen it, and an uproar ensued. The man called the police and even had the doors of the restaurant locked because he thought someone had stolen it while he was eating. After the restaurant search came up empty, he retraced his steps back to Ned's store. Ned told me later that the gentleman had seemed almost on the verge of a heart attack. Ned reunited the man with his briefcase, which turned out to have several hundred thousand dollars' worth of rare coins and stamps in it! Ned told the man that I'd brought the briefcase in, and he said the gentleman wept in gratitude and wanted to present me with a reward.

They then mounted another search: for me! Ned had forgotten that I was only a block away at the movies. After the movie was over, I strolled back into the shop, completely unaware of my new heroic status. Ned spotted me as I walked in the door and rushed over to me. "Where have you been?" he asked. "We've been looking everywhere for you." Then he explained what had happened.

By then, though, the coin collector had already left to return to his home near Tampa, a few hours away. The following day I even earned a small headline in the local paper. My virtue was extolled in the article for returning the briefcase instead of swiping it. A few days later a gift arrived for me, in care of Ned at the store. It was a coin collection worth several hundred dollars—probably several thousand in today's money. It was definitely more money than I'd ever seen in my life.

I couldn't help but notice that all this happened shortly after I'd changed my luck by changing my mind. Of course, it might have been coincidence, but nothing remotely like that had ever happened to me before, and it was the clear turning point in my experience of being lucky. Later I understood that I had stumbled onto some of the other Conscious Luck Secrets, too, all of which you will soon learn yourself.

The coin shop experience was just the first in a lifetime of lucky breaks. Here are couple of others:

When I was a graduate student at Stanford in the early 1970s, I developed a keen interest in helping children eliminate test anxiety. I created a little curriculum of relaxation exercises and guided visualizations to help kids stay relaxed and focused during exams. One day I had a chance encounter with a psychologist named Jim who worked in a nearby office at Stanford. We fell into conversation, telling each other about what we were working on. In that conversation I described a book I wanted to write—a collection of the anxiety-reducing exercises that worked best. I told him I was thinking of self-publishing it to sell to elementary school teachers. He said he had a better idea.

Jim told me that he did some scouting for a publisher, Prentice Hall, and said if I wrote a proposal, he'd show it to them. I rushed back to my office and asked the department secretary if I could use her IBM Selectric after hours. This machine was then the Rolls-Royce of typewriters, because it had a unique device for correcting errors. She said yes, and I sat down the moment she vacated her chair at 5:00 P.M. I stayed up all night writing the proposal and three weeks later had a contract from a major publisher for a book I entitled *The Centering Book*. I got an $800 advance for it, which wasn't particularly generous but felt like a fortune in my ramen-noodle-grad-student life. When the book was published in 1975, my luck served me again, although in a most unusual way.

I had included in the book some simple stretching exercises for children that I had adapted from an ancient yoga book. There was absolutely nothing religious about the exercises, but when my book was published, several far-right fundamentalist groups slammed it and tried to have it banned. Their beef was that yoga was a Hindu cult that somehow posed a threat to children. They accused me of trying to bring Eastern mysticism into schools, a charge that flabbergasted me—all I was trying to do was help kids relax and get focused in the classroom. Another right-wing group put me on a list called something like "The 250 Most Dangerous Thinkers in American History." The list included a lot of people I admired greatly; I was flattered to be in their company. I recall that John Dewey was on the list, as were Margaret Sanger, Thomas Edison, and Thomas Jefferson! A group in Indiana got on the bandwagon by burning *The Centering Book* and a bunch of other education books such as George Leonard's classic *Education and Ecstasy.*

If fellow authors are reading this story, I say to you: Do whatever you can to get your book banned by extremists! If possible, say at least one thing in your book that could even get it burned. I can testify that the publicity value of having your book burned is immense. *The Centering Book,* which the publisher thought might sell ten thousand copies a year (hence the parsimonious $800 advance!), took off like a rocket after it was banned and burned. It sold sixty thousand copies its first year, an amazingly high number for an education book, and continued to sell steadily for the next twenty years.

Prentice Hall ultimately published half a dozen of my books in the *Centering* series, but the best piece of luck was yet to come. *The Centering Book* led to my meeting Katie, my wife now for nearly forty years. Katie was a dance/movement therapist and had bought the book to use in her classes. Several years after she bought the book, she saw a poster advertising an upcoming talk I was going to give nearby. She was the first person to sign up! At that event our eyes met across a sea of people, and that led to a heartfelt conversation of less than a minute, which resulted in a lunch date and a lifetime together. For that alone, I consider myself the luckiest man on earth.

✤

In my work as a clinical and counseling psychologist, I drew often on the stories of Danny's watch and the coin collector to show people how they could change their luck consciously. As I helped more and more people change their luck, I was able to make further refinements to the concepts based on their experiences.

From these experiences, I came to believe that eight main Secrets hold the key to helping people change their luck quickly. I'm going to share those Conscious Luck Secrets with you, exactly as I would if you were sitting across from me in my office. If you will let these Secrets sink in deeply, you'll see remarkable changes in your luck and your life.

Let's begin right now. If you're ready and willing, go to the first Conscious Luck Secret in part 2 and begin the process of changing your luck for the better.

PART TWO

The Four Foundational Secrets:

Making Core Shifts About Luck

1

THE FIRST SECRET

Commit to Be a VLP—Very Lucky Person

When it comes to luck you make your own.

—Bruce Springsteen, "Lucky Town"

Pay close attention now. Let the following sentence sink in deeply: *You change your luck the moment you make a conscious commitment to being lucky.*

Until you make a conscious commitment to being lucky, your unconscious programming runs your luck. Maybe your unconscious mind has only "lucky" programming in it, but I doubt it. You probably wouldn't be reading this if you were lucky all the time. You're probably reading this because you have the feeling that if you were a little bit luckier, a whole lot of good things would happen in your life.

I agree. That's why I'm talking to you like this.

You need to know that it's up to you to change your luck.

That's right: the power rests in your head and your hands. Each of us can make that commitment and bring more luck into our lives. It's actually easy to change your luck, if you will take the challenge of making a few simple shifts in your mind and body. Check into yourself right now and find out if you are sincerely willing to take the challenge of changing your luck.

If you are, take a few deep breaths and get your body relaxed.

I'd like you to make a special kind of commitment right now.

Your First Instruction

Get a pencil or a pen and something to write on.

You're going to write the following sentence, in a specific way that gets it into your subconscious mind. When people pay me big money to help them change their luck, this is the very first thing I have them do. I can't stand over you and watch you do it, so I'm going to trust you to do it exactly as I tell you.

Write out the following sentence. Fill in the blank with your name. Write it only if you are sincere about it.

✤

I, ________________, make a sincere commitment to being lucky, now and forever.

✤

Write the sentence once with your dominant hand. (In other words, if you're right-handed, write the sentence with your right hand.)

Now, switch the pen or pencil to your nondominant hand and write the sentence again. Just scrawl it out as best you can. It doesn't have to be legible to anybody but you. Writing the commitment with your nondominant hand is important, because your nondominant hand is connected directly to your subconscious mind.

Now, switch back to your dominant hand and write it again.

Then, once more with your nondominant hand.

Don't go further until you've written your sentence exactly as I've asked. If you've done it as I've asked, you should have two sentences written with your dominant hand and two written with your nondominant hand.

When you finish, take a break. Go for a walk, perhaps, or get a bite to eat. Take your mind off this for at least a few minutes. It needs some time to sink in.

When you come back from your break, you can go on to the next section or save it for another day. It's up to you.

What Have You Been Committed to Up Till Now?

Ready to continue? Great. Let's talk about the power we have to create our lives.

Whether you realize it or not, you are already demonstrating incredible power to create what you want. The truth of this statement can be seen around you in the fact that you have created the life you have *right now.*

You may not like all of what you've created. You might not think you created it through your choices. You might think it's been "done to you." And while you may not have *consciously* chosen many of the things that you have, nevertheless, it is your power that created it.

You were able to do this because of the power of your commitments. The power of your commitments—both conscious and unconscious—has given you all the things that you now have.

Acknowledge the awesome power that you already have. *If you can create your life one way, you can create it another way.* I found this awareness to be absolutely transformational. It opened me up to a new set of sensations, including the feeling of being in charge of my life.

Here is a personal story that illustrates this point:

> In 1979 I had a life-changing realization during an argument with the woman I'd been with, on and off, for five years. I realized that the argument we were having was not our five hundredth argument—it was our five hundredth run-through of the *same* argument! I didn't realize it until that moment, but we'd been having the same basic argument over and over for five years! A light bulb came on, and I saw clearly that our arguments always followed the same pattern of misery-producing moves. The pattern went like this:
>
> - One of us would fail to tell the truth about something important. For example, she would fail to tell me something she was angry about.
> - I would sense something was "off," but when I would ask her if something was wrong, she would say everything was fine.
> - Tension and distance would grow, and we would criticize each other more as we drifted out of intimacy.

- We would blame each other for a host of things, each of us convinced we were the victim of the other.
- Finally, after a few days or a couple of weeks of escalating tension, we'd blow up at each other with a shout storm of an hour or so. Then the mood would lift, and we'd go back to getting along . . . until the next run-through of the pattern a few days later. Because the makeup sex was so good, I would forget about how painful the previous days or weeks had been.

I stepped back from the process and wondered: *Why would I engage in a pattern like this? Why would I create the same basic argument over and over again for years? Given all the experiences I could be having as a human being, why have I kept repeating the pattern of lying and being lied to, being criticized and criticizing, blaming and being blamed, and thinking of myself as a victim?*

Then, in a rush of realization, I got the answer: These things kept happening because I was *committed* to being criticized, *committed* to being betrayed, *committed* to arguing and lying. I was more committed to my established pattern than I was to having a great relationship. The commitments were obviously unconscious. In other words, I didn't wake up every morning and say, "Today I'm going to create a lot of misery for myself." Something in me was obviously committed to it, though, because it kept happening over and over.

The moment I realized what my commitment was, I felt a huge shift inside. I wasn't a hapless *victim* of my circumstances, I was the powerful *creator* of those circumstances!

Try on that same radical realization for yourself:

If you're lonely, it's because on an unconscious level you're more committed to being lonely than you are to being connected. If you're overweight, it's because on an unconscious level you're more committed to being overweight than you are to being at a healthy weight. Your unconscious commitment to being overweight literally "outweighs" your conscious commitment to being at your ideal weight.

If you're unlucky, it's because on some level (again, usually unconscious) you're committed to being unlucky. I didn't like this idea very much when I first heard it. Maybe you'll be thrilled with it, but it made me mad when I first realized it. I didn't like the reality of gravity the first few times I encountered it, either. But gravity's here to stay, and so is the fact that our results in life will always tell us exactly what we're committed to at our depths.

The very act of becoming aware of our unconscious commitments is an enormous first step in taking ownership of our results in life. It loosens the negative grip of our old patterns and allows us to begin practicing new, conscious habits of behavior. It swings wide the door to claiming our power so we can create the life we truly want.

Savor this point by floating the following idea through your mind. Savor it until you can feel the truth of it in your body:

I acknowledge that through the power of my commitments—both conscious and unconscious—I've created my life as it is now. I now choose to use this power to create my life the way I consciously want it to be.

Now, write those two sentences down on paper, sign it, and date it. Keep it, along with your luck declarations, as a reminder to yourself.

Do not go further in the book until you have carried out the step of writing the two sentences on paper, then signing and dating it.

Wanting to Be Lucky Is a Good Thing

As we were growing up, many of us were made to feel guilty and ashamed about wanting things. We may have been called selfish. Yet unless we ask for what we want, the universe doesn't know what to give us.

It's not until we let ourselves consciously want something that we can consciously receive and enjoy it. Let yourself *want* to be lucky. Go ahead—let yourself want to be very, very lucky.

Now, say out loud, filling in the blank with your name: "Yes, I, ______________, want to be lucky." It's okay if you feel silly or foolish. Do it anyway.

With this statement, you consciously harness the power of "want," which will now help to create more luck.

Go Public with Your Commitments

If JFK hadn't gone public with a commitment to go to the moon, would we have gotten there? Maybe, but we'll never know. What *is* clear is that President Kennedy had the courage to make a public and wildly audacious commitment, braving ridicule and disbelief, to raise the bar of what was possible for mankind. In the same way, you've got to go public with your commitment to being lucky for it to have the most impact.

Begin by feeling the commitment sincerely. You've said it in your mind, you've written it down on paper, and you've given voice to it. Now feel it, breathe into it, let it settle into you. After you feel it, your next step is to go public with it.

Later today, say to someone you know, "I've made a commitment to being lucky."

Notice how the person responds. Such a statement triggers the fears, hopes, and possibilities of other people. Let others have whatever reaction they have to your commitment. Maybe it will inspire them. Maybe it will make them green with envy. Maybe it will stir up their despair and they'll tell you it's impossible. Be sensitive to their reactions, but also know that it's really not your business. Your business is being lucky. When you're on your deathbed you're not going to care what anybody thinks of you. You're going to care about whether you enjoyed life, loved to the max, and had some great luck.

Committing with Joy

You now know that conscious change begins with conscious commitment. But commitment, the way I mean it, is different from other types of commitment you may have experienced. For example, many people think of commitment as an obligation, as something they have to do. When you buy a car, you sign your name and the car is yours. Unless you paid cash for it, you are now obligated to make your payments for a certain period of time. That's "commitment equals obligation." It's one type of commitment, but not the kind that will change your life.

Some people think of commitment as a burden. Let's say you're a coal miner with sixteen children to feed. You go down into that coal mine every day because of your commitment to feeding your kids. Unless you're astonishingly Zen-like in your approach to your coal-mining job, you're likely to feel a sense of burden in your commitment. That type of commitment is perhaps noble, but it's also not what will change your life.

The type of commitment that changes your life is one that is made freely, to support a worthy goal of your own choosing. I believe that the goal of creating luck and abundant good fortune is a profoundly worthy one. If you agree, you're invited now to make the commitment to achieving it.

Here is the way I put the commitment into words: *"I freely and joyfully commit to creating luck and abundant good fortune in my life, now and forever."*

Please say this a few times both to yourself and out loud. Again, savor the concepts and the words, and feel the concepts in your body. Work with it until you feel that it is a sincere commitment that represents something you really want.

Feel a sense of freely choosing the goal. Make it yours.

Commitment Requires Recommitment

When you commit to something, it doesn't mean you'll always be on track—it means you commit to *getting back on track* when you go astray. This concept was made real for me back in the 1970s when I signed up for a seven-day meditation retreat at a Zen monastery.

It was my first time doing anything like that, so I really didn't know what to expect. On the first morning, the other students and I showed up for the first meditation session. The teacher invited us to sit down on the round cushions that lined the hall. He told us to sit, with eyes open or closed, and count our breaths from one to ten. When we got to ten, he told us simply to go back to one. If we lost our awareness along the way (for example, by going off on a train of thought after the fourth breath), we were simply to return to "one" with no judgment and begin again.

"That's it," he said.

He rang a small bell. "I'll ring it again at nine o'clock and we'll break for breakfast." I took a peek at my watch, which informed me that it was just past six o'clock. I took a breath, said "one" in my mind, and began. It was probably the longest three hours of my life—and incredibly valuable. During those hours, I got to experience in excruciating detail all the ways my mind could make me miserable. I would begin my count to ten, then suddenly find myself off on thoughts about some unpleasant experience in elementary school. I'd begin my count again, determined to make it all the way to ten without losing my focus. Next thing I knew, I'd find my chin on my chest and realize that I'd dozed off somewhere around the count of four. So much for my determination. If there was one thing I learned from that first morning, it was how little time I spent in the here and now and how much time I spent worrying about things in the past or fretting about things in the future.

It took me several days of meditation before the light began to dawn on me. It ceased to matter whether I lost the count or not—it was just about being in the present and coming "back to one" whenever I drifted off to somewhere else. I began to feel a marvelous radiance inside and all around me, a glow that intensified as the week continued. By the end of the retreat we were meditating fourteen hours a day, but the hours went by quick as a finger snap.

Recommitting to luck works the same way. When you realize you've fallen back into your old ways of thinking about luck and your old habits of unlucky behaviors, just "return to one"—in this case, the first Conscious Luck Secret—and remake the commitment to being lucky and to practicing the rest of the Conscious Luck Secrets.

Drifting is part of the deal; avoid giving yourself a hard time for it. The power is in the moment of recommitment.

Now that you're fully committed to being a VLP (Very Lucky Person), let's go on to the second Secret!

2

THE SECOND SECRET

Release Your Personal Barriers to Good Fortune

You can create your own luck just like a cloud can create its own rain. You create your own luck by the way you act, think, feel, and talk. If these ingredients you're using to create your luck are distorted, then what will follow is bad luck all the way, like a thunderstorm. But if you're especially careful to watch how you think, then the sweet aroma of good luck will rain upon you almost everywhere you go.

—Mark Benedict, *The Method of Selling*

As any good gardener will tell you, once you plant a seed you must keep the weeds from choking its growth. The process of cultivating good luck is no different. The first Conscious Luck Secret directed you to plant the seed of luck by making a commitment to be lucky. This second Secret is all about clearing away the blocks to Conscious Luck, or what I call your personal barriers to luck that you've been carrying around for years—perhaps your whole life—that have created the results you experience in your life now. Without this essential next step, your desire and commitment to being lucky will have less chance of bearing fruit.

Most people encounter a few barriers and challenges

along the way to getting good luck firmly established in their world. I certainly did. In moving through these barriers in my own life, and in helping others do the same, I came to have a clear picture of the challenges you're likely to face. Take a close look at them with me now. I promise it will save you some grief and angst down the line.

The Big Barrier

I want to show you the biggest one first. Understand it clearly and you eliminate about 90 percent of the hassle factor in life. Here it is: *your conditioned mental patterning.*

Old mental patterns become a stubborn, tenacious, default position that we slip back into quickly if we're not paying attention. To get a consistent flow of good luck in your life, make a point of noticing how often you revert to the old concept of yourself as unlucky. When you notice that your thoughts have gravitated back to the old "I'm not lucky" pattern, gently direct your mind back to your new commitment: I, ________________, make a sincere commitment to being lucky, now and forever.

The trick to making this shift is to be as gentle and accepting as you possibly can. Most people feel the need to stop and beat themselves up when they notice some old unwanted habit taking over. **Nobody has ever beaten himself or herself to genuine wisdom, so don't waste your time trying.** If you do catch yourself beating yourself up, try not to waste more time beating yourself up for beating yourself up! Just notice what you're doing and make the gentle shift back to your new commitment. Let the old thoughts go and choose luck once again.

More on the Art of Letting Old Patterns Go

There's only one good way we can rid ourselves of the old "I'm not lucky" patterns—and it's a bit of a paradox: you get rid of them by *not trying to get rid of them*. To get rid of something is to push it or throw it out of your life. While that may work with a pair of old pants that no longer fit, it won't work with old patterns. Where would you put them? The old pattern and the urge to get rid of it are occurring in the same body and mind. Trying to get rid of your old patterns sets up an antagonism between parts of yourself, like a dog chasing its own tail. One part of the dog doesn't realize it's chasing another part of itself. It goes in circles, nipping at its tail in a futile attempt to catch the elusive quarry. It can be amusing to watch from a distance, but when we're in the role of the dog it doesn't seem so funny. The harder we work to change something, the more it seems to elude us.

Only the act of *benign observation* can free us from doing these futile laps around the perimeter of our consciousness. This is a hypothesis you must test out in your own life to understand fully. In other words, you'll need to experiment with this idea to prove it to your own satisfaction, because it's not something the rational mind can grasp simply by reading the words. In my experience, it will take at least three applications of it in your own life before you begin to understand its power.

To help, let's go deeper. Here's what an act of benign observation actually is: **it's greeting your old "I'm not lucky" pattern with loving attention rather than any form of condemnation.** Herein lies one of the great challenges human beings face. If you pay attention to your thoughts, you will probably notice that you greet a great deal of your life experience with condemnation. *This isn't the experience I ought to be having,* says your exasperated mind as you sit in a major traffic jam on the freeway, late for a meeting. However, it is absolutely the experience you *are* having in that moment, and to condemn it only makes the pressure between your ears build.

What relieves the pressure is a moment of benign observation: the act of accepting that you are having exactly the experience you're supposed to be having. How do you know that it's the one you're supposed to be having? Because it's the experience you actually *are* having.

In those moments of benign observation, you realize that an attitude of "I don't deserve to be where I am" or "I shouldn't be experiencing this" is worthless, and in fact counterproductive, to your peace of mind.

They say that knowledge is power. So, let's recap what you know:

1. You, like everyone, have a default position of old mental attitudes that beckons the newly awakened part of your mind to come back to sleep again in the "safe" confines of your limiting beliefs.
2. To judge, condemn, and find fault with these old limiting beliefs is to keep them locked into place.
3. You need to cultivate a new art form: the art of gently letting go of attachment to your old patterns and shifting into a new commitment to a better pattern—to be lucky, now and forever—as easily as you slip into a perfectly fitting pair of shoes.

The good news is that over time, the consistent repetition of this gentle release of old beliefs, and the conscious recommitment to the desired ones, will create new neural pathways, eventually making your embrace of your lucky life automatic and effortless. This frees your energy and creativity to be put to use in the service of increased abundance and harmony.

As you first practice this, you'll catch yourself after you've thoroughly beaten yourself up for slipping into your old patterns. In this new paradigm, you'll take a deep breath, remind yourself that Rome wasn't built in a day, and recommit to your new patterns. Next, you'll catch yourself mid-beat-up and stop, recommit, and go on. Soon, you'll catch yourself immediately after you find yourself slipping into the old unlucky patterns but before you start beating yourself up, and you'll simply *tsk, tsk* and promise yourself to do better next time. And eventually, the new patterns will become your default. That's when the flow of luck in your life becomes a mighty river.

The Second Barrier: Curses

I know this sounds seriously weird, but stay with me here. I was trained in the scientific method of therapy, in which the subject of curses never came up. Curses, related to folklore and witchcraft, conjure images of black-robed witch figures rattling bones and cackling as they cast spells on their unsuspecting victims—and have no place in modern-day counseling practices.

But I was forced to look again because of the large number of people over the years who've told me they felt cursed in the areas of money, love, or both. A negative energy, seemingly beyond their control, hampered them in their efforts to succeed. As I listened to them carefully and helped them "lift those curses," I came to realize that almost all successful living involves lifting "curses" of one kind or another.

This is because minus the bone rattles, the cackles, and the figure in the robe, a curse is simply a type of limiting belief about our abilities or ourselves (usually absorbed from our parents or teachers or other caregivers) that has become an everyday, always-on, background-noise fact of life, so pervasive we often don't even realize it's there.

Think about it for a moment in regard to your own early life. Were you affected by the curse of not being wanted? According to surveys I've seen, upward of 40 percent of us begin our lives that way. If you count mixed feelings—being wanted *and* unwanted—the numbers go even higher.

And then there are the hundreds of people I've worked with who've told me they felt cursed by the simple fact of their gender—their parents wanted a boy and they turned out to be a girl, or vice versa.

Curses sometimes come to light after a very long period of residing in the unspoken background of relationships. I've had several clients, for example, who've told me hair-raising stories of deathbed confessions that revealed long-standing curses. One middle-aged man I worked with told me of a curse confession his father made to him as my client sat at his bedside during his deathbed vigil. His father suddenly mustered the strength to open his eyes and say, "I never really liked you," before taking his final breath. It took a while for my client to recover from the pain of that moment, but he ultimately came to appreciate his father for his honesty. "I'd suspected he'd felt that way pretty much all my life," he said, "so in a way I was relieved when he finally said it out loud."

Take a minute to reflect on your own life. Where have you felt cursed? And why? Who cursed you? Getting clear about these unconscious beliefs and feelings is a vital part of releasing them. What follows is a technique that will help you move beyond your "unlucky anchors" to an acceptance of your own Conscious Luck.

Identifying and Separating from the "Unlucky Part of You"

As we've seen, the biggest barrier to being lucky is your belief that you're not—whether that belief was formed as a result of perceived curses or other damaging life experiences.

That's right. *There's a part of you that you've never fully examined, and it's keeping you from being fully lucky.* If you'll explore that aspect of yourself—just focus on it now in a special way—it will release its grip on you. Then you'll be free to make a new choice to be lucky.

Here's exactly how to find that "unlucky" part of you. It's the very same process I would use if you were sitting in my office. You may be surprised at how easy it is and also how powerful.

To begin, simply read through this timeline:

THE LUCK TIMELINE

After I finished going to school

When I was in college

When I was in high school

When I was in junior high or middle school

When I was in elementary school

Before I was in elementary school

Before I could walk

Before I was born

Now, close your eyes and take a moment to tune in to your sense of "being unlucky." It might be a vague feeling, or maybe it's a thought in your mind. Somewhere in you, though, you can sense the part of you that feels unlucky. Just give it some attention for a moment.

The First Instruction

With one of your fingers, point to the place on the timeline that corresponds to when you first were aware of being unlucky: in love, in finances, or in any other way. There's no way to know for sure, of course, but just accept whatever answers you get from inside yourself. For example, if you've always felt unlucky, you would probably point to "Before I was born." If you started feeling unlucky when you were in high school, point to that.

Don't go further until you've pointed at one or more of the phrases on the timeline.

Instruction Two

Now, think for a moment about your parents and your grandparents. Most of us who feel unlucky have either parents or grandparents who felt unlucky also. By being around them, we picked up their attitudes unconsciously. (If you were adopted and know your birth parents, think of them as well as your adoptive parents. If you never knew your grandparents, think of any stories you've heard about them.)

Below you'll see two lines that read "My parents" and "My grandparents." With one of your fingers, point at either or both of these lines if you feel your parents and/or grandparents felt unlucky. You may have had a father who felt lucky and a mother who didn't, or vice versa. Same with your grandparents. If you feel one of your parents or one of your grandparents felt unlucky, then still point to the line. There's no way you can know for sure—just go with your impression. If you don't have the sense they felt unlucky, just wait a moment. Don't point.

MY PARENTS
MY GRANDPARENTS

Breaking the Grip of the Past

Now, I'd like you to do something incredibly important for changing your luck.

Look at the original timeline again. Point to a place on it that corresponds to when you felt unlucky. Point with your finger.

Now, while pointing at the timeline, say the following phrase out loud: **"That was then."**

And then touch your chest with that same finger as you say, **"This is now."**

You may feel resistance to doing this. Thoughts like *This is stupid* or *This will never work* may come up. You're disturbing deeply ingrained parts of your psyche, and this can activate the part of your brain and personality that is invested in the status quo—whether that status quo serves you or not.

We'll discuss this dynamic again later, but for now, whenever those feelings of fear, discomfort, or self-ridicule come up, take a deep breath and acknowledge the part of you that's trying to keep you safe, and assure it that you will be even safer—and happier—at the end of this process. Then let the negative thought go.

Do this part of the exercise at least ten times. Say, **"That was then"** as you point at the timeline, then touch your chest as you say, **"This is now."** It's important that you physically touch your chest when you say, **"This is now."** Make sure you say it out loud. I suggest ten times, but you can do it dozens of times if it feels right to you to do so.

Then, I'd like you to do something similar while thinking about your parents and grandparents. If you feel that any of your parents or grandparents felt unlucky, point to those lines as you say, **"That was them,"** and touch your chest with that same finger as you say, **"This is me."** Do that at least ten times.

After you finish doing this, take a break. Come back later or another day for the next session.

You may feel freer after this exercise, or if you experienced resistance, you may continue to feel very uncomfortable. You may even want to put this book away and stop the process of cultivating more luck.

Don't do it. It may feel good in the moment, but it will

set you back in the long run. As I mentioned above, when we commit to change things in our lives, those forces that are comfortable with "the way things are" act strongly and swiftly to discourage us from our newly intended goals. This can come from inside: self-sabotage from fear of success, "upper limits" issues, or simply fear of change. When we make a conscious effort to change, everything standing in the way of change is activated. We must prepare ourselves for this onslaught and position ourselves properly, or like a big wave, it will wipe us out.

This releasing process gets easier and easier as you continue, and I promise you, any discomfort you feel along the way will be a small price to pay for the rising tide of good luck you'll experience as a result.

Here's a great story to illustrate the power of this process: I remember one time a man in his early thirties came to see me because he couldn't seem to stop spending money. Between disastrous investments and a gigantic spending spree, he'd burned through almost $2 million. With $250,000 left in his account, he was desperate to figure out why this was happening.

"First of all," I asked, "how did you make the money?"

He said, "I didn't make it. I inherited it from my father."

I immediately felt an internal alarm go off. "And what was your relationship like with your father around money?"

That's when I learned about the "curse" his father had put on him. The man's father had been a financial genius who'd told his son repeatedly that he was stupid, was hopeless with money, and would never be successful. "I suffered from the crime of being like my mother," my client told me. "The thing I remember him saying most often was, 'You'll never amount to a hill of beans!'"

And that was precisely how the young man's life had been playing out—until his father died unexpectedly in his fifties, leaving my client with more than $2 million, a heart full of resentment, and the limiting belief that he didn't deserve to have that money.

So what did he do to express his rage at his father and stay true to his early programming? Waste all that money that his father had carefully earned all those years. What's more, the curse played out, as curses so often do, with my client completely unconscious of the dynamics at play.

I helped my client lift the curse using the timeline techniques, "That was then, this is now" and "That was him, this is me." What his father thought about him and money was no longer relevant and was outside his control anyway: his father was dead, and the money was gone. The important thing for my client was to ground himself in the here and now.

After freeing himself from his past, my client, although he didn't make the millions of dollars back, was able to earn a satisfying living and get on with his life—plus he had a $250,000 nest egg!

✤

Now that you're letting go of old patterns and clearing the pathways for luck, we're going to focus next on a specific personal barrier to luck: shame. In the next chapter, you'll learn not only how to release shame, but how to transform the space it occupies in your body—as an unwelcome squatter—into an attractor for luck.

3

THE THIRD SECRET

Transform Shame into a Magnet for Abundance

The shame that tormented me was all the more corrosive for having no very clear origin: I didn't know why I felt so tainted, and worthless, and wrong—only that I did.

—Donna Tartt, *The Goldfinch*

Perhaps you were raised, as I was, to harbor a great deal of shame inside you—shame about the size or shape of your body, or about something you did that angered or hurt someone else, or about something that was done to you. Your shame may be hidden so deeply inside that it's difficult to detect it. Or you may be able to feel it consciously right now, by scanning your body with the microscope of your awareness.

I feel shame as an old lingering sting, an unpleasant warmth in my legs and hips. I also feel it as a clench somewhere in the center of me, as if I've swallowed something too big to go down and yet too deep to come up.

What's worse, I experience shame not only as something I've done that's wrong, but also as something that has brought disgrace to my family.

I have memories of a certain look on both my mother's and grandmother's faces—one that communicated more than disappointment. Their look told me I was causing shame in them; something I'd done had brought their own unworthiness to the surface. The look meant I should be doubly ashamed: I'd done something wrong *and* I'd caused them to reawaken an old feeling of inferiority.

That feeling of shame piled on top of shame was unbearable to me as a child, and I had no choice but to conform myself to their way of being so that the feeling would go away and they would love me again. Still, a tiny spark of awareness in me felt that something was wrong with their way of seeing the world. I wondered if I was really all that bad.

Though I have only a few specific memories of feeling shame early in my life, there must have been many more. My parents and grandparents appeared to feel a great deal of shame—it seemed to infuse them. So much so that as a young man, I felt guilty about feeling less shame than they did. It was much later in life that I figured out the true depth of my family's shame and the impact it had on me.

A Legacy of Shame

For a long time, I was unconscious of my shame as a physical sensation. Even though I'd helped other people become aware of the feeling of shame in their minds and bodies, I didn't get in touch with that toxic emotion hidden in my own body until my mother died, in 1990. I was forty-five years old. My older brother, his daughter, and I had gone to Florida to sort through the contents of my mother's house in preparation for selling it. In the process, I came across a greeting card from a member of my mother's church group that had been stuck behind a framed family photo. I stood for a moment debating whether I should read it but decided there was no longer any need to protect my mother's privacy.

The card, written in spidery old-fashioned handwriting, said, "You must come out of the house. You can't continue to hide there. I know your pregnancy and the death of your husband fill you with great shame but we're here for you. We don't care what's gone before or that you're a single mother."

My brow furrowed. *Why was my mother so ashamed of my father's death?* The family story told to me by my mother and brother was that before I was born, my thirty-two-year-old father had come down with a rapid-onset kidney disease and died suddenly. This event, I had been informed, had plunged my mother into deep grief and a severe anxiety about money, but I don't remember anyone ever mentioning shame. Up until reading the card, I'd never questioned that story, but now I flashed back to the time I'd been talking with an M.D. friend of mine about our fathers. When I'd told him the story of how my father had died, he'd said, "Hmm, that sounds like some kind of poisoning to me." I hadn't really taken his comment in fully, but now, with a sickening thud, everything suddenly fell into place: *Oh my God, I wonder if my father committed suicide and everybody has been stonewalling around that ever since.* Though I knew I'd probably never be able to confirm the facts surrounding my father's death, just like that, my mother's shame made perfect sense to me.

While I was still reeling from that shock, another alarming realization crashed over me: the pregnancy they were referring to was *me*. Clearly, I had been *pickled* in shame in utero.

The fetus that grew to be me was composed of cells literally soaked in the biochemicals of disgrace—and that shame had to still be present in my body.

Standing in the living room of my mother's house, I turned on my awareness and did an internal scan. Sure enough, I could feel a burning sensation all over my body, but it was more concentrated in my face and down in my legs and buttocks where my mother used to apply the switch on me. (The worse the offense, the higher up on my legs she'd hit me.) The sensation was definitely connected to a feeling of shame. It had been there all along, in the background, and I hadn't known it.

Once I woke up to shame's presence, I worked on releasing it through a process of seeing it, feeling it, and ultimately accepting it, and over time, I made good progress. Still, I never imagined I could take something so thoroughly unpleasant as that physical sense of shame and turn it into a major force contributing to my abundance.

A few years after my trip to Florida, I found a way to transform shame into a magnet for luck. I felt as if I'd tapped into a mysterious new power in the universe. And almost from the moment of this discovery, I saw a greater flow of good fortune into my life.

My Discovery

At the time of my shame-to-luck discovery, I was already reasonably good at manifestation. My net worth was probably around $5 million. That was fine, and I was certainly not complaining. However, I had a conscious intention of creating a

$20 million endowment for our foundation before I popped my clogs. (The Foundation for Conscious Living gives grants and scholarships to support research, resources, and outreach in the fields of conscious living and loving.)

I wasn't sure how I was going to get to my $20 million goal. I'd changed my luck and harnessed the powers of manifestation to get where I was, but I didn't know any other "tricks" that would get me the rest of the way.

One rainy Saturday I was loafing around, pondering one thing and the other, when a question appeared in my mind: *What do I already have inside me that I can use as a larger attractor-field for luck?* I'm not sure where this question came from or how I knew to ask it like that, and I suppose it doesn't really matter. What matters is the magnificent results it produced.

A split second after I registered the question, I was flooded with an answer that changed my life. The answer didn't come in the form of a word thought or a picture. The answer was something I could feel: a vast part of the inner field of myself suddenly illuminated, as if it were lighting up for the first time. I immediately recognized the parts that illuminated as the places in myself where I felt the old shame from childhood. Then an insight appeared in my mind: THIS *is what I can use as an attractor-field for greater luck!* The nerve endings that once had been dedicated to feeling shame could now be tuned to a higher purpose: attracting abundant luck, wealth, and happiness.

I was filled with a deeply satisfying wave of bliss as I felt this vast territory of my inner self begin resonating with this new purpose. Waves of blissful inner sensation continued on and off for days thereafter, as this new purpose lit up larger and larger areas of my inner self.

After that experience I could feel, almost like a gravitational pull, the $20 million fortune drawing me toward it. I still feel it as keenly in this moment, even though I'm so much closer to the goal than I was when I first switched on the constructive power of my old shame machinery.

Over the course of the next few years, I often checked in with the parts of myself that had been dark and full of shame to find that they were still light—in both senses of the word. This new inner glow and buoyancy was a constant in the background, in the same way the shame sensations had been, but with a decidedly more beneficial effect: luck seemed to stream toward me from all directions.

One of my most impressive strokes of shame-transformed-to-luck came in the form of a twenty-five-year-old stockbroker wearing a Hawaiian shirt and flip-flops (with braces on his teeth, no less) who showed up one day in our office. Katie had met him through her parents and had invited him to tell us about a special investment opportunity. A start-up company called Software.com had developed a useful bit of software that made email go faster. We were offered the stock at $3 per share. I lacked the technical savvy to understand the investment fully (and to be honest, the tender age of the stockbroker didn't inspire my confidence, either), but Katie felt differently, and fortunately her wiser head prevailed. We purchased the stock and later cashed out when it was close to $100 a share. This contributed significantly to our net worth—and our ability to fund our foundation.

That's my story. Now let's focus on your story, with the

intention of putting the power of your own shame machinery to work for you as a magnet for luck. We'll start by exploring shame and your relationship to it.

Shame 101

Our shame becomes toxic when we internalize messages from others that don't serve our health and well-being.

—Jessica Moore, therapist and coach

In the last chapter, we looked at limiting beliefs and how they form personal barriers to luck. Shame is another barrier to luck because it makes us feel undeserving of good fortune—love, happiness, and success. Shame also limits luck because it keeps us living in the space of the past, echoing around in the field of shame and not being present in the here and now where luck takes place.

Many people equate shame with guilt, but there is a difference:

Guilt is feeling bad about something we've done.
Shame is feeling bad about who we are.

Guilt is like a dog bite, acutely painful and unpleasant, but we can alleviate it by apologizing, making amends, and committing to do better going forward.

Shame is like a hot woolen blanket on a humid day—heavy, suffocating, and miserable. Though it may be caused by the same actions that produce guilt, shame is guilt gone underground, causing us to perceive ourselves as fundamentally flawed in some way that can't be changed. What's worse, like curses, this feeling of being defective morphs into a constant background experience and so becomes unconscious.

For the purposes of this book, I'm not going to deal with guilt. There are many fine books on the topic you can read. Instead, I'm going to focus on shame: how it's acquired and stored in the body and, most important, how you can transform it.

What you may not know about shame is that nobody is born with it. It's instilled in us. This is a good place to compare us with our cousins the chimpanzees, with whom we share a close genetic link. In fact, research shows that the chromosomal difference between humans and chimps is ten times smaller than that between mice and rats!

This means chimps have almost identical muscles and nerves to the ones in which we human beings feel shame. However, if you try to get a chimp to feel shame, you've got your work cut out for you.

Let's say you want to instill some shame in a chimp, so you sit down with three chimps at a table. You put a chunk of banana on the table. One chimp, a big guy we'll call Charlie, snatches the chunk of banana and eats it. The two smaller chimps express their upset with the unfairness of this action. They shriek and squeal and bounce up and down. You look the banana snatcher in the eye, give him your most baleful scowl, and say, "Shame, shame, *shame* on you." Then you put another chunk of banana on the table. Charlie immediately snatches it and stuffs it in his mouth. This shameless act of "me first" banana grabbing triggers another episode of shrieking and bouncing by his friends. "Shame on you, Charlie," you say again, hoping he will hang his head and see that his impulsive acts are causing pain to the rest of his colleagues.

Be prepared to spend a very long time at the table before you start seeing any results; in fact, if we leave you and come back next month, you'll probably still be shaming Charlie and he'll still be snatching bananas.

In contrast, it's very easy to get humans to feel shame. Shame is almost always introduced after you're old enough to be up and around and interacting with the people close to you. Most of the time, the people who instilled the shame in your mind and body did so for a noble reason: they wanted to keep you from repeating behaviors that would get you into trouble. They didn't know how to do it any other way than by shaming you.

The big problem is that shame becomes buried in our psyche and lingers in our body. We often still feel shame decades after such childhood incidents as being caught "playing doctor" by a parent, or stealing change from our father's dresser, or wetting the bed.

Whatever the cause, here's the bottom line: There is no organic shame built into you; there's no muscle or nerve that science can point to and say, "These are the shame muscles and nerves." You were trained to feel shame, and that feeling gets lodged in the muscles and nerves of your body. Then, like a low-grade fever, shame zaps your luck and your energy for life—unless you learn how to deal with it effectively.

It's time to take the first step.

The Shame Paradox

What you resist not only persists, but will grow in size.

—Paraphrased from the work of Carl Gustav Jung

As you discovered in the last chapter when we explored releasing your personal barriers to luck, one of the ways your negative emotions and limiting beliefs keep their grip on you is by making you think you should try to get rid of them.

Shame is an especially uncomfortable emotion—one that most people avoid feeling at all costs. If we do consciously experience shame, we're usually desperate to relieve the pain it creates and struggle mightily to free ourselves from its grasp. The problem is that fighting with shame keeps you engaged with it. Shame will cheerfully shadowbox with you for a lifetime. The more you wrestle with shame, the stronger its grip on you becomes. Shame gets to stay in charge as long as you're trying to get rid of it.

That's reason number one I don't want you to declare war on shame: it doesn't work—in fact, it makes it worse. In the same way that the second Conscious Luck Secret asked you to change your approach to releasing your barriers to luck—whatever they might be—this secret asks you to try the same thing with shame: just acknowledge that you have it and quit trying to eliminate it. Say "hello" to any shame you feel and then simply let it be.

But don't stop there. After you let it *be,* I want you to let it *become,* which brings us to reason number two you don't want to get rid of shame: Just as I did, you can use all the territory that's been claimed by shame for magnetizing abundance. Shame is just a placeholder until you learn how to let it become a massive capillary bed of attraction for luck. So let's begin the process of putting shame to work for you rather than against you.

Transforming Shame into Luck

Now it's time for us to do the body-centered, experiential process that will liberate you from the grip of shame. It's best to do this process seated comfortably, at a time when you can give your full attention to it.

THE CONSCIOUS LUCK SHAME-TRANSFORMING PROCESS

1. Start by closing your eyes, then taking a few deep breaths and tuning in to your body—the sensations you feel, your weight on the chair, bed, or floor. As you relax into awareness of your body, notice any feelings of shame present inside you. Don't get caught up in the emotional aspects or the reasons for your shame, simply do a scan of your body for any feelings of shame present.

   Like the constant flow of thoughts in your mind, shame comes to you unbidden. You woke up one day, perhaps a lifetime ago, and it was there. You didn't have to ask for it. Perhaps you've felt burdened by it and have wanted it to disappear from your body, but it has remained with you anyway.

2. Take another deep breath and gently focus on the presence of shame in various places in your body. For exam-

ple, you might feel that it extends from your waist down through your legs: your buttocks, thighs, and calves. Part of that might be because, like me, that's where you were often struck physically while you were being shamed, or it might relate to feelings you have about your sexuality, or it might be about something else entirely. Perhaps you feel shame in your chest or stomach. Or in your hands or your face. It's not important whether you can feel it clearly right this moment or not. It might be below the surface of your conscious awareness. Even if you don't feel the physical sensation of shame at this moment, recall the general dimensions of it as you've felt it in the past.

The physical component of shame needs to be at the forefront, because that's your avenue to the psychological part of it.

3. Notice any tension, tingling, or other sensation in your body thoroughly and deeply. Let your attention rest on each area of sensation for about the length of three easy deep breaths, about fifteen to twenty seconds, until you feel some sort of a release—at least a little.

   Most people don't get a release because they're not willing to feel the shame deeply enough. Any troublesome feeling that you're willing to focus on and allow to exist will transform into open space.

4. Now, imagine that open space—whatever its size—filling with light. You may experience this visually or as a felt sensation in your body. Let the light pour into the spaces

once occupied by shame like clear, sparkling water displacing muddy water in a glass.

Continue the process for another few breaths: feel the physical sensation of shame anywhere you find it in your body until it releases into openness, then fill that space with light. Take a few minutes to savor the new experience of light, open space where there was constriction and heaviness before.

You were once rich in shame. It was like an inheritance. It came to you spontaneously and absolutely free of charge. Shame once lit up areas of your body, and now those areas are being illuminated with something new and better. You've heard the saying "Like attracts like." Now, feel the truth of that saying in your body. A vast field of richness has opened inside you, and this inner richness attracts outer richness in the form of abundant money, health, purpose, and love. Breathe in this new richness, accept it, and let it make its home in your body.

5. The final step in this process is to infuse your being with the opposite of shame: self-love. To do this, bring to mind someone in your life whom you love deeply—a spouse, a child, a parent, a friend, or a pet. Feel the love in your heart for that special individual in your life. Let that feeling expand until it fills your internal space completely. Take another deep breath and now switch your focus from your loved one to yourself. Don't let any thoughts about your faults or mistakes sidetrack you—keep your focus on your body. Just turn the stream of your love onto yourself and let it flow, drenching you. Let the love soak in.

6. When you feel complete, take a few deep breaths, and keeping your eyes closed, gradually start moving your body: wiggle your fingers and toes, do a gentle neck roll, stretch your arms and legs. Then when you're ready, open your eyes slowly. Take a little time to transition into your normal activity.

At the beginning of a symphony concert, the oboe player sounds a tone and the rest of the orchestra tunes to it. In the same way, you've just sounded a tone of good luck throughout yourself, allowing your nerve endings to tune to that new note.

New Life, New Rules

Starting today, I want you to declare a new day—with new rules—in your body. The places where you used to feel shame are now open spaces in which luck and abundance flow freely.

Here's the truth of the matter: You have the power to make up new rules for your life, provided those rules do not conflict with existing laws of the universe.

There is no law in the universe that condemns you to feeling shame all your life. I promise you that. There is no law that says you cannot be lucky. This is your time to choose the rules for your relationship with luck. Based on the Conscious Luck Secrets you've learned so far—and the ones still to come—I invite you to make up a new rule that says: *I attract and enjoy wonderful luck.* I urge you to choose good fortune as the governing rule of your universe.

Choose now.

And so it is.

IMPORTANT NOTE

Dear Reader, this is the point at which the collaborative portion of *Conscious Luck* begins—notice the "we" voice going forward. Read the Authors' Note at the beginning of the book to refresh your memory about this lucky partnership!

THE FOURTH SECRET

Have Luck-Worthy Goals

Luck is simply the advantage a true warrior gains in executing the correct course of action.

—R. A. Salvatore, *The Halfling's Gem*

To create luck on a consistent basis, you need to give luck plenty of good reasons to visit. The fourth Conscious Luck Secret focuses on goals, an often unrecognized way to attract luck. Our experience, both in our own lives and in our work with clients, has taught us a powerful lesson: *Luck chases worthy goals.* In this chapter, we're going to ask you to take a clear-eyed look at your goals, so you can give luck the very best reasons to visit.

Begin with This Question

It's safe to assume you're reading this book because you want more luck in your life. But what do you want that luck to help you achieve? The first question to ask yourself is this: *If I were totally, completely lucky, what would I be doing or what would I have that I'm not doing or don't have right now?*

For example, you might say:

If I were lucky, I'd be making a six-figure income as a coach (or writer or musician or . . .).
If I were lucky, I'd be living in a beautiful house on the beach.
If I were lucky, I'd be living happily with the woman/man of my dreams.
If I were lucky, I'd be able to give substantial funds to support an orphanage in Africa.

The person in the example above has four goals: a well-paid and rewarding livelihood, a house on the beach, the love of a wonderful partner, and the fulfillment of endowing a worthy cause.

Who decides what your goals should be? You do. No one else.

We can tell you, though, that to turbocharge the luck-attracting quality of your goals, choose goals that are luck-worthy. This means goals that:

- Are deeply meaningful to you
- Light you up and allow you to do what you most love to do
- Are beneficial to you personally *and* to other people at the same time

Remember, your true goals are not your "to-do list." To-do items are usually the front-burner—often *urgent*—actions that overshadow the *important* long-term objectives you want to achieve in life. Most of us lose sight of the truly significant things we want to do and devote all our energies to taking care of our daily needs and "putting out fires" of one kind or another.

Your true goals bring you closer to why you specifically are here on this planet—your contributions to make, your lessons to learn, your talents to develop and share, and the unique experiences your soul craves.

To complete the foundation of Conscious Luck, we need to get clear on the goals we'd like our luck to help us achieve and, if necessary, adjust them to be more luck-worthy.

Here's your job right now: Carefully select at least three goals you can place out in front of you on the horizon and write them below.

My first goal:

My second goal:

My third goal:

You're welcome to have more, but we'd like you to choose at least three.

Done? Great. Now it's time to give your goals the Conscious Luck sniff test.

Luck-Worthy Goals Are Deeply Meaningful to You: What Do You *Really* Want?

The first requirement of luck-worthy goals is that they are deeply meaningful to you. This secret requires that we get real with ourselves about what we *really* want in life. Many of us have no clear idea of what's truly important to us. If you ask most people, "What do you want?" common responses are, "More money," or, "More time freedom," as if these goals were ends in themselves. In truth, it's not the money or time for its own sake that we want, but what having it allows us to do.

So if having more money and time freedom are among the goals you wrote above, try taking the next step and ask yourself, *If I had more money or more time freedom, what would I do then?*

Would you travel? Would you spend more time with your spouse, your children, or your aging parents? Would you open an animal shelter or work with disadvantaged youth? Would you write the great American novel? The truth is that we want money or time—or both—so that we can pursue what's meaningful to us.

To take your self-discovery to an even more powerful level, ask: *If I had all the money and time I could possibly want, what would I do then?*

We know it's tempting to keep reading, but really, stop, put the book aside, and take a few minutes now to reflect on this question; then put on paper whatever answers come to you. There's no need to act on your answers yet—just let them percolate up from inside you and write them down. For the next day or two, keep this question in mind, and in your quiet moments let it continue to do its illuminating work.

Answering this question will help you identify your deepest motivations, passions, and causes and will point the way to your true goals—the ones that give luck good reasons to visit.

Luck-Worthy Goals Light You Up: The Conscious Luck Heart Meditation

The second requirement of luck-worthy goals is that they light you up and allow you to do what you most love to do. What's meaningful to you and what you most love to do are entwined like the twin strands of the DNA molecule. To zero in on this aspect of your goals, we offer a body-centered approach that we call the Conscious Luck Heart Meditation. In this meditation, you'll experience how your goals resonate in your heart. This will help you separate out any "should" goals that someone else may have told you were good for you but that don't align with your deeper sense of self.

THE CONSCIOUS LUCK HEART MEDITATION

1. To start, review the goals you've written down for a few minutes.
2. Then, sit comfortably in a place where you won't be disturbed. Close your eyes and take three deep, slow breaths in and out.
3. Now, in your mind, not out loud, say the first goal on your list. Let the words drop into the stillness of your inner world like a stone into a pool and feel the vibrations resonate in your body. Pay special attention to how these vibrations feel in your heart area.
4. Do you feel expansion or contraction in your chest? Do you feel like laughing? Do you feel excited? Bottom line, does your goal light you up?

If not, that goal's not going to draw luck to you. Play around with the goal—adjusting it till it creates the whole-body smile we're going for. If you can't, put it aside and continue with the next goal on your list.

5. Repeat this process with all the goals you've written down. Note the ones that pass the test.
6. You can prioritize your goals using the same process. Go through your goals again and pay attention to which goal is the most expanding, the most exciting. Make that goal a priority in your life. This means no matter how busy you are, commit to completing at least one to-do item on your daily list that brings you closer to that goal.

As simple as this meditation seems, it's a potent tool for identifying how you truly feel about your goals. When your heart and mind are united in support of your goals, luck can't help but assist you.

Luck-Worthy Goals Benefit You and Others: The Universe Winks

I believe we are here to do good.

—Armand Hammer, industrialist and physician

The third requirement of luck-worthy goals is that the fulfillment of your goals benefits you *and* other people. Purely selfish goals simply don't attract as much luck or inspire as much support from other people.

When the positive effects of achieving your goals ripple out beyond just you, you put yourself in the flow of larger, unseen forces that uphold the natural growth and order of the universe.

One of those unseen universal forces is the evolutionary advantage of compassion, empathy, and kindness. You may be surprised to learn that Darwin did *not* coin the phrase "survival of the fittest," which has been used for over a century to justify self-interest and besting others as the most effective survival strategy. In fact, Darwin, in one of his later books, *The Descent of Man,* describes how natural selection favors those who show greater compassion and kindness because it leads to more cohesive and supportive communities, which are more likely to flourish. "Survival of the kindest" paints a more accurate picture of Darwin's philosophy and, in a larger sense, how the universe works.

When your goals line up with this compassionate quality of the universe, you become eligible for a universal quid pro quo—a "You scratch my back, and I'll scratch yours" arrangement—in which all sorts of cosmic "coincidences" and unexpected support show up. We call this phenomenon "the universe winking at us."

Daniel Poneman, a sports agent based in Chicago, told us about his own spectacular wink from the universe:

> For as long as I can remember, I've loved basketball—playing it, watching it, and discussing it. At fourteen, I even started my own basketball blog where I posted my analysis of the performance of all the high school players in the Chicago area, as well as across the state. Within two years, there were hundreds of college basketball coaches from all over the country reading my

blog and asking me questions about players they were looking to recruit.

That got me thinking: *What if I could help young athletes—who were never going to be pros and might not have the opportunity to go to college—get basketball scholarships to junior, Division II, and small colleges?* To do this I organized showcases where the coaches from those types of colleges could come and see the lesser-recognized players play.

My idea worked! As a result of those showcases, hundreds of kids—mostly from the inner city—went to colleges around the country. What's more, many of those graduates have returned to their communities as coaches, teachers, and mentors, which is really needed.

Though I loved what I was doing, eventually it was time for me to start earning a living. I wasn't sure what I wanted to do, but when a few of the athletes I worked with ended up becoming pros and asked me to represent them, I reluctantly became a sports agent.

The problem was I just didn't fit into that competitive, often cutthroat, industry. The solution was to start my own agency, but that was out of the question—it required far more money than I had or could ever come up with on my own. I resigned myself to being an outlier in my field.

Then something extraordinary happened: I was introduced to one of the country's richest investors. He'd heard about my nonprofit work and wanted to support me. First he invested in a documentary some friends and I were making about Chicago basketball players titled *Shot in the Dark*, and later he invested the money for me to start my own agency.

Shot in the Dark was a great success, and today my agency is thriving. I know I was lucky, but I also believe that when you set out to help people, not expecting anything in return, somehow it comes full circle.

Harness the Power of Altruism

Even if you don't subscribe to the notion of a universe interested in aiding you personally, having goals with an altruistic component is still very useful on a physiological level for creating Conscious Luck.

Recent studies in the field of positive psychology show that the instincts of caring, cooperation, and the desire to help others are indeed hardwired into our brains. According to researchers using advanced imaging technology to monitor brain function, our pleasure centers—the same areas of the brain that respond when you eat a dessert or receive money—are activated when we give to others around us. We can harness the drive created by altruism's powerful biological rewards to help us achieve our goals.

Our colleague Jack Canfield, author of *The Success Principles* and a cofounder of the Chicken Soup for the Soul series, related an interesting example of this that happened at one of his workshops. Jack had asked a course participant to come up to the front of the room and to think about accomplishing an important goal of hers, but to focus *only on the benefit to her* from achieving the goal. Then, using an applied kinesiology technique called "muscle testing" (which is based on psychoneuroimmunology, the study of "the interaction between psychological processes and the nervous and immune systems of the human body"), he pressed down on the woman's outstretched arm to see if this thought strengthened or weakened her system. Her arm went weak.

Next, he asked her to focus on how achieving the same goal would *benefit the other people* in her life. This time when he pressed down on her arm, it was rock solid.

It was the identical goal, but the thought of the wider good she could create by achieving it was more strengthening and empowering. Jack has repeated this same demonstration many times since then, always with the same result.

You don't have to be like Mother Teresa or join the Peace Corps to enlist the luck-attracting quality of altruism. Simply identify and focus on the altruistic aspects of your goals—whatever your goals may be. For example, let's say one of your goals is to purchase a Tesla. If you focus exclusively on how having a Tesla will benefit you—how snazzy you'll look behind the wheel of such a beautifully designed car, how you won't ever have to go to a gas station again, the big tax credit you'll receive, and so on—it's not as empowering (or luck attracting) as focusing on how having a Tesla will also benefit others: reducing carbon emissions, having a safer car for your family, modeling action in line with your convictions to your children and your community, and so forth.

So, working toward something for yourself, combined with the intention to contribute to others, enhances your ability—spiritually, emotionally, and physically—to achieve your goal. It also places you in the fast lane where luck is concerned.

Luck-Worthy Goals in Action: Putting It All Together

Katie Anderson, a young woman who recently attended a training at the Hendricks Institute, is an impressive human being by any standard. CEO of her own company, Katie has received national and international recognition for her leadership in the social impact sector. When we heard her story, we knew it was a great illustration of the three criteria of luck-worthy goals and how they bring success:

KATIE'S STORY

I have learned this . . . that if one advances confidently in the direction of his dreams, and endeavors to live the life which he has imagined, he will meet with a success unexpected in common hours.

—Henry David Thoreau

I've been called "lucky" a lot in my life, but for a long time I was defensive about it. I felt it discounted all my bravery and courage—and my hard work. In my mind, luck was a freebie, something unearned. But in the last few years I've learned that when I operate from a deep creative place inside me to come up with outcomes in which everyone wins, what I call "dockings"—magical synchronicities and "impossible" occurrences—happen. Great good luck follows me around now and I welcome it!

I was one of the first in my family to go to college.

I wanted to be a doctor or a lawyer, something prestigious and impressive. I chose doctor and majored in biomedical studies. But in my junior year I got restless. I didn't want to spend the next ten years in training. I wanted to start my life *now.* I began reading books about personal growth, including Napoleon Hill's *Think and Grow Rich.* That's where I first heard the term "entrepreneur."

I remember that moment so vividly. *Wait,* I thought, *I can create anything I want in my life?!* The passion to forge my own career path was born and the entrepreneur dream seeded. From then on, I knew I wanted to throw all my energy into building my own dreams using my own creativity.

I decided on real estate investing and after graduation got a job as a commercial real estate appraiser. It was perfect to prepare me for investing—plus I got to earn while I learned. For the next few years I lived frugally and learned the ropes. I had student loans and credit card debt but, living paycheck to paycheck, I couldn't make much headway in paying them down.

One night I was eating dinner out and couldn't help noticing the couple at the next table. They looked like a pair of light bulbs—so lit up from within. They radiated happiness. I wanted that same kind of light for myself.

We struck up a conversation and they told me their passion was competing in triathlons to raise money for charity. I'd heard of triathlons but had never considered doing one. I was immediately intrigued by the challenge of it, and the next day I signed up for my first one, raising money for lymphoma and leukemia research. That was when my life started expanding. I saw a big world out there, so much bigger than just me and my career and my money.

I met amazing people training for that first triathlon—cancer survivors and people with family members battling cancer—who simply wanted to help others. It was deeply inspiring and cemented my decision to make fund-raising triathlons a part of my life.

My involvement in triathlons also led me to people who would be important in my career. The first was a fellow triathlete I'll call John. John had a water conservation company and was looking to expand his business near Houston where I lived. He offered me a sales job. I looked at the market for his services and saw it was wide-open. But I didn't want to be an employee—I wanted to be an entrepreneur. So I told him I would work independently on straight commission. He was delighted.

Some months earlier, I'd left my appraiser job and begun real estate investing, but now I dove into the world of saving water. Our target market was big apartment complexes, where we could significantly reduce both water usage and cost by making simple repairs and improvements and earn a percentage of the future savings on the reduced water bills.

I believed deeply in what we were doing and thought it would be a snap. I loved the threefold win of John's business model: conserve one of our planet's most precious and endangered resources—water—save property owners substantial sums of money, and generate profits for our business.

Yet four months later, I hadn't made one sale. I had only $400 left in the bank, but I refused to give up. Inside I knew it was going to work. If it came down to it, I decided, I would take a bartending job at night, leaving my days free to sell our services. I would do whatever it took. I wouldn't quit.

Two days later, I made my first sale—a $45,000 contract that paid me 10 percent. Two weeks after that, I brought in a $250,000 sale. I became the rainmaker at that company for the next four years, earning a consistent six-figure income.

Even so, I continued to live extremely frugally, paying off all my debts and even managing to sock away $75,000 in savings. At the three-year mark, my pay was cut. Management told me I "was making too much money." I wasn't happy, but I was still making a lot of money, so I stayed. A year later, my pay was cut again—"You can't make more money than the boss." That was the final straw.

I like to say the universe turned up the heat. It was time for me to make a change. I gave in my notice.

Over the next few months, many people called me to offer jobs, partnerships, and pieces of start-ups. I was tempted yet found myself unable to commit to any of the offers. I finally realized why. I saw that in a year or two or ten, I'd be back at the same fork in the road—with someone else calling the shots or potentially putting a cap on my creativity or earnings. I wanted full control of my future.

I turned down the offers and contemplated my next steps. I was drawn to water conservation and had my own ideas about it but was unclear what to do. One evening, I was on a call with a friend who was listening to me try to figure it out for the umpteenth time. He interrupted me to ask, "Katie, would you be willing to start your own company?"

I paused and really took his question in. I visualized the entire range of possibilities, from the worst—total failure, the loss of my savings, having to start over—to complete success—boatloads of money, awards, the deep satisfaction of contributing to the field—and everything in between. My heart leapt as I fully accepted all the potential outcomes of my decision. "Yes!" I answered, and felt my whole being surge with fear and elation. That entrepreneur seed had finally sprouted.

I spent the next week coming up with the name of my company. It was my first lesson in listening to myself about my business. I asked friends and family for suggestions. Nothing felt right. Finally, I threw the lists away and asked myself, *What are you doing?* The answer was clear: *I'm starting a company to save water.* Save Water Co. The URL was available. Bam! That was it.

I called two friends from college, single guys who had started careers in fields totally unrelated to water conservation and plumbing, and asked them if they wanted to work for my new company. I told them they'd be working hard for very little money. To my surprise, they both said yes.

Since we had no track record to point to, for our first project I approached the owner of an apartment complex and offered to do the work for free if he would pay us half the water bill savings we produced. He agreed. We had two weeks to repair and retrofit 218 units, starting the following Monday. I planned to use a big part of my $75,000 nest egg to finance it.

Until this point, I'd been a salesperson but had never done the physical work of fixing leaks and changing out showerheads and toilets. Neither had my two friends, Save Water Co's first and only employees. That weekend, we took a crash course in plumbing with my dad, taking my parents' master bathroom apart and putting it back together until we knew what we were doing.

The two guys showed up to work at the project on Monday morning while I tried to drum up our next sale. The guys' learning curve was steep and scary: the first day, they completed one unit—217 to go. The second day, three units. I felt a whisper of panic. At that rate, we definitely weren't going to get this job done on time. I had to jump in and help. So for the next twelve days, all three of us worked. Hard. As we went along, our speed increased. We finished the last unit five minutes before the deadline. The job was a resounding success—the next water bill on that complex showed a 44 percent savings!

Still, I couldn't keep financing the company and

knew I needed more funds immediately. A banker I'd met through my charity work came to mind. Five years earlier he'd said to me, "You're going to be CEO of your own company someday."

I called him. After exchanging hellos, I said, "Well, you were right! I'm the CEO of my own company. May I please come over and talk about money with you?"

He dealt with much bigger companies than mine, so he referred me to an associate who specialized in small businesses. The associate and I sat together for an hour and a half and I explained what I was doing. He asked about my background and experience and then asked, "Do you have any assets for collateral?" I didn't. Then he asked to see my business plan.

"Business plan? I don't know what that is," I answered. My heart sank a little.

He looked at me appraisingly for a few seconds, saying nothing, and then turned to his computer, punching numbers into his keyboard.

When he turned back to me, he said, "I can authorize a two-hundred-fifty-thousand-dollar loan. Will that be enough?"

Smiling broadly, I said, "Yes!"

When I told my friends about the loan, they were incredulous. "That just doesn't happen," they told me. That was when my outlook about luck started to change. By traditional standards, I clearly wasn't qualified for a loan, but this banker had obviously seen something deeper, something deserving of a chance.

There was one small problem: for the loan to go through, I had to put up 20 percent of that money—$50,000 I didn't have. But I trusted that my luck would hold. And it did. Over the next few days, I closed two paying deals with one client who deposited his $49,700 down payment directly into my account. Bingo. Loan secured.

Four years later, we're debt-free. I have thirty-seven employees, and we expect to reach more than $7 million in billings this year. In 2015, *Forbes* magazine named me one of their "30 Under 30" to watch, and in 2017, I won the Cartier Women's Initiative Award, one of only seventy women in the world to receive this honor since its inception in 2006.

With every decision I make, I ask myself, *How can this be a win for everyone involved?* That includes the client, the company, the employees, the community, and the environment. This level of problem solving requires an enormous amount of imagination and outside-the-box thinking. So far, I'm happy to say I've been almost 100 percent successful. This uniquely creative challenge is why I feel so fulfilled at the end of each day. I no longer worry about making enough money. My wealth is an automatic by-product of me using my innate talents.

And luck? I say bring it on! I'm willing and available—committed—to being the luckiest person I can be, because what that means for me is honoring the true, authentic expression of myself and drawing from my internal well of creativity.

Final Words About Goals

The fourth Conscious Luck Secret tells us that to change our luck consciously, it's crucial to take time out of our busy lives to clarify our true aims and goals. It's also extremely rewarding to inquire deeply inside to determine what you most love to do, what motivates you at your most fundamental depths, and what you feel most passionately about expressing in the world.

Whether you've done a lot of work on goals or none at all doesn't matter. Discovering your true goals is not a one-and-done thing. As you grow and change, your goals may grow and change, too. Start today by simply asking yourself the questions in this chapter and listening deeply for your answers.

When we follow the thread of our dreams and desires from the superficial to the deeper levels of our hearts and minds, we automatically uncover more juicy, exciting goals. This is a reward in itself, but it's also like a neon sign flashing—signaling the forces of luck to take notice.

✣

Using the four Foundational Secrets, you now have the direction you need to make luck-changing shifts at the core of your being:

- Commit to being lucky
- Release your personal barriers to luck
- Transform the shame you hold in your body into a magnet for luck
- Revisit your goals to make them worthy of luck

These four Secrets allow you to build a firm foundation for Conscious Luck.

The next chapter begins part 3, where you'll learn the four Daily Living Secrets: practices you can do each and every day to make luck a living, breathing reality in your life.

Onward!

PART THREE

The Four Daily Living Secrets:

Luck-Changing Practices to Do Every Day

5

THE FIFTH SECRET

Take Bold Action Consistently

Put "P" before the word "Luck" and you have the password to the attainment of all your desires.

—Walter Matthews, *Human Life from Many Angles*

While the fourth Conscious Luck Secret involves giving luck a *reason* to visit, the fifth Conscious Luck Secret is about giving it an *opportunity* to visit—as many opportunities as possible.

You create an opportunity for luck to appear in your life by taking bold action: trying something new, being more spontaneous, taking risks, and asking for what you want—in short, getting out of your comfort zone. And the more of these bold actions you take—think of them as cosmic lottery tickets—the greater your odds of a lucky outcome.

In this chapter, we'll look at the different ways to start a lucky streak and how to overcome one of the biggest obstacles we face in doing so: fear.

We'll also let you in on another facet of this gem of a secret: the remarkable luck-generating power of giving. When all else fails, take a break from focusing on yourself and your own projects and get out there and support somebody else. This seeds the clouds, emotionally, physically, and spiritually, for a downpouring of luck on your highly fortunate head!

Mix It Up a Little

Without awareness, there is no choice.

—John F. Barnes, physical therapist, lecturer, and author

Trying something new—an important catalyst for starting a lucky streak—can take different forms. You can vary your routine, say yes to new ideas and methods, or tackle things you're afraid to do. The simplest and least daunting way to try something new is to change up your daily activities.

A lot of us go about our lives on autopilot. We get up at the same time, get ready for work in much the same way, drive to and from work along the same route, talk to the same people, eat the same kind of food, and so on. Often this is because we've discovered the most efficient way to do what we need to get done. But just as walking repeatedly along the same path over time can wear a deep groove in the ground, taking the same actions day after day puts us in a rut. Even if it's a good, healthy, efficient rut, it still limits our chances to be lucky.

Decide today to mix it up a little: go to a different store for your groceries, try a new style of clothing or a new hairdo, go to an unfamiliar restaurant, sample an ethnic cuisine you've never tried, or pick a new vacation destination. Breaking out of your familiar routine increases your exposure to different people, ideas, and outlooks.

Moving through life with this new, more adventurous awareness is refreshing and energizing, as Gay shares with this experience:

> I realized I'd been brushing my teeth with my right hand for my entire life, so I decided to switch hands and brush with my left for a month. I wondered what would happen if I changed this one little thing. It was amazing how much it woke me up! Plus, I found a real joy in that act of consciously brushing my teeth rather than automatically going through the motions while thinking of something else. It was very helpful in creating a more mindful experience.
>
> Another thing I did was try to take a different route to the office each day. There was one obvious way to go, but whenever possible I'd drive around another way or take an alternate street and backtrack. I just kept jiggling with my reality. I found it valuable for coming to my day in an awakened state—I was more alert and open and noticed more of what was going on around me.

When you take a new path on your daily walk, or drive an alternate route to work or school, you'll not only see new things, you'll see through new eyes, with a heightened perception of the world around you. This increases your luck by allowing you to spot chances and openings you'd likely have missed while on autopilot.

Dr. Richard Wiseman, psychology professor at the University of Hertfordshire and one of the first positive psychology researchers to delve into the phenomenon of luck, uses a wonderful analogy to explain the powerful benefits of varying your routine:

> Imagine living in the center of a large apple orchard. Each day you have to venture into the orchard and collect a large basket of apples. The first few times it won't matter where you decide to visit. All parts of the orchard will have apples and so you will be able to find them wherever you go. But as time goes on it will become more and more difficult to find apples in the places that you have visited before. And the more you return to the same locations, the harder it will be to find apples there.
>
> But if you decide to always go to parts of the orchard that you have never visited before, or even randomly decide where to go, your chances of finding apples will be dramatically increased. And it is exactly the same with luck. It is easy for people to exhaust the opportunities in their life. . . . But new or even random experiences introduce the potential for new opportunities.

Another benefit of mixing it up is that when you decide to consciously try new things, you're more spontaneous and open to out-of-the-box ideas. You give yourself permission to be creative.

The universe is in a perpetual state of creative ferment. Astronomers calculate that approximately three thousand new suns are born every second! Imagine what you can accomplish by opening yourself up even to just a fraction of that mind-blowing stream of creativity, rather than always sticking with the tried-and-true.

When you start saying yes to those creative ideas and inspirations—not only is life more fun and interesting, but you also maximize the possibilities that auspicious events will occur for you.

Say Yes

> *Being spontaneous is . . . calmly trusting that, whatever the outcome, you will have a positive if challenging experience that will lead to greater self-awareness and success.*
>
> —Sylvia Clare, *Trusting Your Intuition*

If you've ever taken an improv class, you know the cardinal rule is to say yes to whatever the audience or fellow cast members throw your way—"You're an octopus at a restaurant, an Eskimo in a sauna, a nervous flier on your first transatlantic flight"—and run with it. "Going with the flow" takes you out of your head, disallows overthinking, and brings you to some unexpected places. When you follow little impulses, not knowing exactly where they'll lead, magic can happen.

Steve Sisgold, speaker, coach, and author of *Whole Body Intelligence,* shared a story of a time when saying yes and going with the flow had a stunningly serendipitous result:

> In 1996, Steve, in the mood for an adventure, booked a trip to India. After landing in Mumbai, he took a bus to Pune, where he hoped to take meditation classes and see more of the "real" India, off the beaten tourist path.

On his first night in Pune, as he strolled through the streets, reveling in the exotic sights, sounds, and smells, Steve noticed that there were cows everywhere: walking wherever they pleased, lying down in the street and on the sidewalk, eating whatever presented itself. He was struck by how free and "in the flow" the cows were. He called this free state "cow-consciousness" and decided he would try it himself the very next day.

The following morning, Steve began his go-with-the-flow / cow-consciousness experiment. Wandering around a market area, following his inner promptings, he looked down an alley and saw a man waving at him and beckoning him over. Steve hesitated, unsure of the wisdom of meeting with strangers in foreign alleys. But the man seemed harmless, and feeling an internal nudge to walk toward him, like a good cow, he did.

When Steve reached where the man was standing, the man spoke two words, "Dalai Lama," and pointed to the scooter parked next to him. His message was clear: *I'll take you to see the Dalai Lama.* Steve was more than a bit skeptical. Although it was a strong desire of Steve's to meet the Dalai Lama—one of his heroes—he knew the holy man didn't live anywhere near Pune. What was the likelihood? Still, Steve took a second to check in with himself and immediately had the impulse, *I'm on an adventure, why not?*

Sending up a prayer, Steve climbed onto the scooter and took his seat behind the stranger. They made their way through the crowded streets, eventually leaving the city and entering the countryside. After about ten to fifteen minutes, the man slowed the scooter and pulled it over to the side of the road, where in the adjacent field, Steve saw a group of about twelve monks dressed in saffron and maroon robes, sitting in a circle. There, in the middle of the circle, was the Dalai Lama!

When His Holiness saw Steve walking toward him, his face broke into a broad smile and he started laughing. And as Steve joined the circle, the Dalai Lama, still smiling, nodded at him. Steve said later it felt as if the Dalai Lama knew that he was coming.

Although the Dalai Lama spoke to the group in his native tongue, his interpreter translated his message for Steve: Be authentic, true to who you are, and remain nonviolent, even when confronted with violent behavior. His Holiness also reminded the group that we all deserve love and that we *are* love. This had a deeply healing effect on Steve, who had been suffering emotionally after a recent breakup. The Dalai Lama's powerful words, as well as the memory of that unexpected and intimate gathering, stayed with Steve long after his trip to India was over.

There were so many decision points in Steve's journey where "regular" Steve would have pulled back and relied on his established ideas of how things work or what he believed was possible, thereby missing one of the high points of his life.

Being too fixed in your approach or too narrow in your focus makes you overlook opportunities you aren't expecting. You may be thinking, *Wait, isn't focus a good thing?* Of course it is. What we're referring to is rigid, what you might call "contracted," focus—a focus so sharp that you are no longer present to the rest of your environment. People who can maintain both a strong focus *and* broad awareness simultaneously have been shown to have more luck.

Evidence of this comes from British psychology professor Richard Wiseman, whom you met earlier in the chapter. Dr. Wiseman once did an experiment by asking self-identified lucky and unlucky people to count the number of photographs in a newspaper.

The unlucky people, looking intently for the photographs, took an average of about two minutes to come up with their total. The lucky people took only a few seconds. That's because Wiseman had printed a large message on the second page that read, "Stop counting. There are 43 photographs in this newspaper." The unlucky people, looking only for photos, didn't see the message. The lucky people were more all-inclusive in their scan. Wiseman's conclusion:

> And so it is with luck—unlucky people miss chance opportunities because they are too focused on looking for something else. They go to parties intent on finding their perfect partner and so miss opportunities to make good friends. They look through newspapers determined to find certain types of job advertisements and as a result miss other types of jobs. Lucky people are more relaxed and open, and therefore see what is there, rather than just what they are looking for.

This part of the fifth Conscious Luck Secret, being open to the world around you and letting it unfold organically, may take some time to master—especially for control freaks and those of us prone to anxiety—but it's worth it. Beyond improving your good fortune, you'll find it will boost your quality of life in all areas.

Which leads us to the next and most challenging way to try something new: doing things you're afraid to do.

Go for It

Go out on a limb. That's where the fruit is.

—Jimmy Carter

Starting a lucky streak requires action—you've got to play to win, remember?—and the most powerful luck-activating moves require leaving behind your comfort zone and taking a risk.

Risks don't have to be daredevil or physically dangerous. They can be as commonplace as striking up a conversation with a stranger, attempting a new skill, venturing out on the dance floor, or asking for something you want. These actions feel risky because you're opening yourself up to the possibility of failing, feeling foolish, or being rejected—conditions that make most people's blood turn to ice water in their veins.

Why are we so afraid to fall short or look dumb? Because of our survival wiring. In our cave days, if we failed at our given roles, or were considered inferior or undesirable, or were rejected by a potential mate or the tribe, it meant a lower quality of life—or even death. Now that's scary stuff!

And although failure, humiliation, and rejection are no

longer physical threats to our lives, we still react to them from a primitive part of our brains and do everything possible to avoid experiencing them. This avoidance, which gives us a sense of safety, also keeps us stuck in a low-luck zone.

We love what Susie Moore, the author of *What If It Does Work Out?*, says about playing it safe: "Feeling fear and stepping backward rather than taking a step forward may feel like a safe option, but it actually isn't. You're not adding more to your life or being more powerful in life. The actions we take in our lives [that require courage] are always our proudest moments."

Here are three ways you can overcome this type of fear and its accompanying paralysis:

1. **Respond rather than react**

   Learn to distinguish when the fear you feel is based in reality rather than concocted by your brain's Stone Age mechanisms.

   If a snake is about to bite your ankle, that's a good thing to be scared about. That's the natural purpose of fear—to make you jump out of the way. If there's really something threatening your safety, do what you need to do to protect yourself.

   But if the "snake" is coming from between your ears, hampering you rather than protecting you, that's a different thing. Then it's a good idea to learn how to ignore our brain's automatic panic reaction. Treat that internal flare of fear as if it's a car alarm going off down the block. We register the sound, but since we know that 99.9 percent of the time there's no crime in progress, we don't get rattled or call 911. We usually don't even feel any emotion, except perhaps a slight irritation at the noise, and we're able to continue doing what we need or want to do despite the alarm sounding.

2. **Use the breath to switch the body's biochemistry**

The breath, the body's best regulator of emotions, is a good tool for releasing the physical tension we feel when afraid.

Fear can be defined as "excitement without the breath." When we're scared or anxious, we tend to contract physically. We hold our breath or breathe shallowly. This stokes the physiology of fear, creating even more agitation.

Fear also makes us see the world differently. People having an anxiety attack get tunnel vision and can see only a tiny portion of what's going on, which causes them to view the world as a frightening place. Fear creates more fear and traps us in a particularly negative feedback loop. As Sophocles said, "To the man who is afraid everything rustles."

Fortunately, you're only three deep breaths away from feeling more fearless. Studies show that it takes only three healthy, long, slow breaths to activate the body's parasympathetic response and begin to chase the "stress chemistry" out of your system.

If you can remember to breathe deeply in distressing situations, it's possible to turn the negative experience of fear into the positive experiences of excitement, alertness, and pleasure.

3. Face your fear

There are times when our fears get the better of us. Our logical minds can give us evidence that there's nothing to be scared of, but the terrified child within doesn't buy it. Sometimes the only way out of fear is through it. Both of our spouses had situations where confronting their fears head-on was the best solution.

Carol's husband, Larry, saw the movie *King Kong* when he was eight years old. The film absolutely terrified him. After having nightmares for a week, he couldn't stand it anymore. He decided he would just have to go find King Kong and let the worst happen. He was tired of worrying about it. That night, after everyone was in bed, Larry sneaked out of the house (located in the Colorado foothills) and into a nearby clearing, ready to meet the monster. For more than an hour he sat on a rock, looking up at the surrounding mountains, waiting for King Kong to come over the nearest peak so that he could fight him. But nothing disturbed the stillness of the night and Larry eventually went back to bed—his fear of King Kong completely and permanently dissolved!

For many years, Gay's wife, Katie, was afraid of flying. Her work requires travel, so there's no escape from getting on planes. She relied on breathing techniques, which made her more comfortable on flights, but nothing she tried took away the distress completely. At one point, she decided she'd had enough and made the radical decision to go skydiving. It worked! Jumping out of an airplane at twelve thousand feet zeroed out her fear entirely. Today she flies around the world without giving it a second thought.

To paraphrase Shakespeare, the coward dies a thousand deaths, the hero only one. When you realize that your fears and worries create more suffering than the actual events you shrink from, "bearding the lion" becomes the only option.

Twenty Seconds of Insane Courage

Sometimes all you need is twenty seconds of insane courage, just literally twenty seconds of embarrassing bravery, and I promise you something great will come of it.

—Actor Matt Damon's character, Benjamin Mee,
in the film *We Bought a Zoo*

By now we've established that to start a lucky streak, you need to be brave enough to take risks. The good news is that you don't have to be brave *all the time,* just in isolated moments when it counts. The openings for stepping up are usually only seconds long, so if you can muster your courage in a well-timed burst, you're over the hump. Carol's "twenty seconds of insane courage" allowed her to ask for what she wanted *and* not walk it back, which changed the course of her life:

CAROL'S STORY

Fortune favors the bold.

—Latin proverb

In the early days of the Chicken Soup for the Soul series,

my dear friend Marci Shimoff secured the contract to write *Chicken Soup for the Woman's Soul* with Jack Canfield and Mark Victor Hansen. Marci knew that I had majored in literature in college and I loved doing research, so she hired me to help find material for the stories in her book.

I went to the library—this was in the days before the internet and Google—and spent several hours combing through magazines and newspapers, looking for articles about inspiring women. I found a few but was stumped how to write up a story that wasn't just a plagiarized version of the original piece I'd found during my research. In a light bulb moment, I decided to track down the women and interview them, then write their stories in the first person, as if I were experiencing the events myself. Marci loved the idea and agreed to pay me at a higher rate for my writing work. More research yielded the women's phone numbers, and voilà, I was in business.

Although I was a voracious reader, I had never really written anything before. Even so, I found I had a talent for ghostwriting: I could ask the right questions during an interview to draw out the important details and then write easily in someone else's voice.

Marci loved the stories I sent her, and when *Chicken Soup for the Woman's Soul* was published in 1996, I was overjoyed to see three of my stories in print. The book was an immediate *New York Times* bestseller that ended up selling millions of copies. As a result, Marci made a lot of money. I was thrilled for her, but I couldn't help thinking, *Marci made so much more money as a coauthor—curating, compiling, editing, and marketing the book—than I did writing stories for the book. What am I doing wrong?* It felt like a waste of time to think this way, so I let it go.

Not long after, I received a phone call from a man named Dr. Marty Becker. Dr. Becker was a veterinarian, but not just any veterinarian—he was the *Good Morning America* vet, appearing regularly on national television. He was also a syndicated pet columnist, as well as one of the world's foremost experts on the human-animal bond (or The Bond," as he called it). Marty was going to be a coauthor of *Chicken Soup for the Pet Lover's Soul,* and Marci had recommended me to Marty as a writer/researcher for his book. I absolutely love animals, especially dogs, and Marci thought I would be a perfect fit.

On our call, Marty told me that for months he had been soliciting pet-lover stories through his column and his lectures on The Bond at veterinary schools around the globe and had amassed a large number of story submissions. He asked if I would consider working on the book, the way I'd worked with Marci. The first step would be for him to send me some samples of the stories he'd collected.

The package arrived and I remember pulling out the top five stories of the six-inch stack of stapled sets of pages inside the box. I sat at my desk and read them with growing excitement. When I finished, I sat back and stared into space, my mind whirling. Of the five stories, four were what I called "killer stories." These were elevens on a scale of one to ten—stories that leave you cheering or choked up or laughing or feeling uplifted and inspired. I definitely wanted to work on this book.

Marty and I were scheduled to talk later that day. I sat

down to do my afternoon meditation program and remember thinking, *I don't want to be just a researcher/writer for* Chicken Soup for the Pet Lover's Soul, *I want to be a coauthor.* It was such a strong desire. How could I make that happen?

An hour later, the phone rang. It was Marty. We exchanged pleasantries and then got down to the topic of the book. "How did you like the stories?" Marty asked me.

Here was the moment of truth. I surprised myself by saying, "Well, there's good news and bad news. Which do you want to hear first?"

Startled, Marty hesitated, then said, "Uhh . . . good news?"

I said, "This book is going to be off the charts! These stories are absolutely amazing, and I'd love to work on this project with you!"

"That's terrific!" he said. "So, what's the bad news?"

"I don't want to be an editor/researcher," I told him. "I'll work with you only if I can be a coauthor on the book."

After an uncomfortable few seconds, Marty finally said, "You're kidding, right?" But when I didn't respond, he continued, "I'm sorry, but there's no way."

"I understand," I replied. And I did. It was a lot to ask. At that moment, I felt my stomach tighten as all my fears came rushing to the front of my mind: *I need the money. Will I ever get another job offer as good? Am I being foolish? Greedy? Maybe I should just say I'll do it anyway.*

Instead I said something that changed my whole future. "Well then, I'll just repackage the stories and send them back to you. Should I use the return address on the box?"

It was one of the bravest things I've ever done. I was willing to walk away and not settle. I was going for what I truly wanted.

Again, the line was silent for a beat, then Marty said, "Wait . . . can't we work something out?"

"I don't know," I replied, "can we?"

We talked for another fifteen minutes. I told him all the reasons making me a coauthor was a good idea: after working on Marci's book, I knew what made a story sing, and as an over-the-top pet lover, I knew what pet lovers would respond to. I would dedicate myself to the book full-time and give it my all, making his participation in this book significantly easier. With his crazy-busy schedule, he needed me!

My points hit home. We finished the call agreeing that we would meet ASAP and that Marty would consult with Jack and Mark about making me a coauthor and coming up with a royalty percentage.

The rest, as they say, is history. After some negotiating, I became a coauthor on *Chicken Soup for the Pet Lover's Soul,* which soared to the top of the bestseller lists. This led to writing five more books in the Chicken Soup series, which then led to writing self-help books with motivational speakers and thought leaders, including Gay Hendricks! Five of those books have been on the *New York Times* bestseller list, including one at the number one spot. In the years since then, my financial situation, as well as my skills as a writer, has blossomed.

From the outside, it might appear that I was lucky. But I know that my luck began with a moment of knee-buckling fear—and the courage to overcome it.

In your own life, don't worry about always being brave; focus instead on recognizing the windows of opportunity and hurling yourself through them. Failure isn't permanent, but coulda-woulda-shouldas are. And here's an encouraging fact: success breeds success. When you successfully survive one risk, it makes it easier to do it again.

Of course, you'll need to follow up your lucky breaks by applying yourself with focus, enthusiasm, and persistence. That's how you create lucky streaks.

There's one more part of this secret that's a departure from what you might expect. Your good fortune can also be jump-started by forgetting about it every so often.

Giving to Others Breaks the "Luck Vapor Lock"

> *Help others without any reason and give without the expectation of receiving anything in return.*
>
> —Roy T. Bennett, *The Light in the Heart*

Have you ever heard of vapor lock? In older cars, sometimes the liquid gasoline turned to vapor, creating a blockage in the gas line, preventing the engine from getting the fuel necessary to run. Something similar often happens to people: pressure—usually self-created—builds up inside and blocks the positive outcomes we want until we can release that pressure.

The final part of this Conscious Luck Secret is an extension of something we learned in the last chapter—the power of giving. Even if you already have luck-worthy goals that benefit others, there's still huge value to forgetting about yourself sometimes and asking, "What can I do right now for someone else?" Especially when you've hit a wall and nothing seems to be working.

On days like those, Carol's colleague and friend Chellie Campbell, author, speaker, and one of the most positive people on the planet, says she dedicates time to serving others. She starts by looking at her list of contacts and asking herself, *Who can I help today?* She enrolls in someone's classes, buys someone's product or service, looks for people she can introduce for their mutual benefit, calls friends and neighbors and asks if there's anything she can help them with, writes testimonials and reviews for deserving businesses, books, and service providers. In short, she does her very best to help others flourish in any way she can. The result? Chellie writes:

> *What happens when I do this seems almost magical. As I help others, I help myself. When I make someone else happy, I become happy. My day brightens as I brighten someone else's day. And then the dam breaks. Whatever was holding me back, disappears. Referrals start calling me "out of the blue." People call whom I've never met, referred by people I've never met! Money and good start flowing to me again.*
>
> —Chellie Campbell, *The Wealthy Spirit*

Gay shares another example of this dynamic:

> Some years ago, I had a phone call with a client who was having trouble with depression. I could tell from his heavy exhales and barely enunciated speech that the

man was in a dark place. In a moment of inspiration, I asked him, "Have you seen anything recently that could use improvement or that you might do for another person?" There followed a long silence. Finally, the man said, "Yeah, when I came home today, I noticed that the patio of the elderly lady who lives in the apartment downstairs was dirty. She's at an age where she can't operate a broom anymore." Perfect. I told the client that I'd stay on the line while he went to sweep that area. The man was gone for a while, and when he came back on the line, I could hear immediately he was breathing normally—his inhalations and exhalations were fuller and more balanced. This opening in the man's dark armor allowed me to begin to work with him to address the deeper issues that were holding him back.

Giving for the sheer joy of it breaks the "vapor lock" on your luck, your love, your happiness, your money supply, your energy, and your creativity. Receiving and giving are part of the same cycle. You need both.

✤

The fifth Conscious Luck Secret tells us that the *quantity* of your luck-creating endeavors are as important as their *quality*. To successfully harness the winds of luck, you must raise your sail—by taking bold actions or finding ways to give to others—and keep raising it over and over again.

In the next chapter, we'll explore how the company you keep can make or break your ability to improve your fortune.

6

THE SIXTH SECRET

Find Your Lucky Tribe

Don't sleepwalk through your social circles—be intentional about how you spend your time, and who you spend it with. You're ultimately responsible for shaping the environment that will shape you.

—Amanda Roosa, writer and photographer

To change your luck, you may need to wean yourself from hanging around unlucky people. Specifically, those people in your family or friendship network who are engaged with you in an unconscious "we're unlucky" conspiracy.

The word "conspiracy" comes from the Latin *conspirare,* meaning "to breathe with." You may discover, as we did, that you spend too much of your time breathing the same air as unlucky people. To change your luck, form a good-luck conspiracy by spending more time taking in oxygen with lucky people.

Researchers have found that the people you're around repeatedly have a measurable effect on everything in your life, from your health and longevity to your morality and worldview, and most especially on your mind-set, which has been shown to be inextricably linked to your luck.

Emotions Are Contagious

A major characteristic of a bad-luck conspiracy is that its members tell victim stories to each other. A victim story is one that portrays the storyteller as the victim and someone else as the perpetrator. A longtime bartender told us that what he'd learned from all those years behind the bar is that people love to complain about their bad luck. Think of those folks who like to drown their troubles and tell their tales of woe to anyone who'll listen—this is just one common example of a bad-luck conspiracy. There are many others.

Around tax time, for example, it's easy to get into a conversation about how taxpayers are the victims of the IRS and the government. Gay caught himself doing this once upon a time, on the occasion of writing a check for $285,000 to the IRS:

> At that point, it was the biggest chunk of money I'd ever had to pay the IRS, and I found myself circulating a dozen different variations of the same victim story through my mind. In the story, I was always the hapless, hardworking guy who was being forced to fork over a small fortune to the government so they could spend it on big-boy war toys and roads to nowhere. I entertained a few of my friends with my story, and in return they were happy to tell me a victim story of their own encounters with the Arch-Perpetrator, the IRS.
>
> Fortunately, enlightenment dawned in the form of an intervention by my genius wife, Katie. She inter-

rupted me in the middle of one of my IRS rants and gently inquired, "Shouldn't we be happy that we made so much money that we're paying $285,000?"

After a few moments of brain freeze as my mind tried to grapple with this previously unthinkable idea, I realized I liked her story a lot better than my own. Hers was a story of delight and empowerment. Mine was a whiny effort to prove what losers we all are in the war with the evil empire. In my story of victimhood, the heavy-breathing Darth Vaders of the IRS always came out on top.

I changed my story on the spot. In my new story, I was glad to be paying that much, because it celebrated a fabulous year during which we'd had a bestselling book, a couple of major television appearances, and other successful ventures. Instead of griping about how the government was going to spend the money, Katie and I put our hands on the check and blessed it to its highest uses.

That wasn't the end of the matter, though. I still had some work to do to rid myself of the tendency to think like a victim. It was difficult work, too, because it involved kicking the addiction to relationships based on mutual victimhood.

You may find it useful to apply the remedy I used. I went through my address book with one question in mind: *Do I ever swap victim stories with this person?*

I was amazed and rattled to discover several people in my acquaintance who fit this category. A couple were family members, others were friends, but they all had

> that one quality in common—they would agree with me, and I with them, that we were victims of one thing or the other: the government, the past, ex-spouses, our families of origin, or the vagaries of the weather. Our mutual victimhood was the currency we exchanged and the glue that held the relationship in place.

We recommend you try this technique, too. Go through your phone contacts, your Facebook friends, your work directory, any list of people with whom you're in contact, and with each person, close your eyes and feel into the energy between you. Within seconds, it will be abundantly clear who is a good-luck conspirator and who reinforces your patterns of unlucky thinking and behaving.

You may come across friends and family in this process who aren't people you share victim stories with but who you feel, in some way, don't support or celebrate your growth and success. Maybe they feel threatened by you changing or don't approve of the direction you want to take in your life. It doesn't matter why—these people also don't qualify as members of your lucky tribe, at least for now.

Moving On(ward and Upward)

> *You cannot change the people around you. But you can change the people that you choose to be around.*
>
> —Anonymous

When you've identified all those who are *not* in your lucky tribe, the next step in your journey to being lucky is to skillfully separate yourself from these people and develop new, more positive connections and associations.

This doesn't have to mean rejecting or completely severing ties with those who aren't in your lucky tribe. But it does almost always require spending less time with them, at least until you're strong enough to 1) resist the old toxic patterns of sharing victim stories; or 2) not feel discouraged by their lack of support and approval for your goals and dreams.

This can be tricky if the people you need to spend less time with are old friends or even your own family! Business owner and motivational speaker Glenn Agoncillo told us how he was able to achieve escape velocity while maintaining his important close relationships:

> I come from a huge extended family: my mother has twelve brothers and sisters and my dad has five. I grew up in San Diego with about a hundred of my mother's relations—cousins, aunts, and uncles—living within a ten-mile radius of my mother, my brother, and me. Most of these relatives lived in large, multigenerational households, and their philosophy about how to live life was loud and clear: Get a good job, find an apartment (big enough to share with your family members), and stay there until you retire or die—whichever comes first.
>
> Following their example, I went to nursing school, but right before graduating, I realized that medicine wasn't for me. I'd worked in an insurance company to pay for my schooling and found I was good at it—more than that, I loved it! I wanted to continue working in the insurance field.

My family was horrified. They argued I would make much more money as a nurse, but for me, it wasn't about the money, it was about what made me happy. I thought it might be best to put some distance between us so that their disappointment and disapproval wouldn't create a true rift.

Plus, their life vision didn't align with mine. As much as I loved my mother and brother, I didn't want to live in an apartment with them for the rest of my life. I was afraid that if I stayed, the gravitational pull might prove too great, so I decided to move to Long Beach, about a three-hour drive from San Diego.

I went to my mother and explained that I wanted to move for the same reason she'd wanted to come to the United States from the Philippines when she was young: I wanted to branch out and grow. It took courage, as I wasn't sure if she would still be angry or even ostracize me. But she heard me, understood, and gave her blessing. I believe it was speaking from that deeply authentic place inside me that made the difference.

After the move, I began driving back to San Diego every other weekend to visit my family and close friends.

That was eighteen years ago. I've created a wonderful life in Long Beach *and* I'm still very close to my family. My brother is one of my best friends, and my mom is one of my heroes. I'm godfather to both my nephews and adore spending time with them. I still drive back every other weekend. I feel I have the best of both worlds.

Glenn's story makes clear that leaving situations that may be hazardous to your luck doesn't have to mean leaving your family or friends behind. It can mean honoring the best of what you have, without being limited by it. What's more important is what you're going toward, which is finding your lucky tribe—surrounding yourself with those who support and celebrate your growth and success.

Bloom Where You're Planted: Finding Your Peeps

> *Find people who help you feel more at home in your heart, mind, and body and who take joy in your joy. Find people who love you, for real, and who accept you, for real. Just as you are. They're out there, these people. Your tribe is waiting for you. Don't stop searching until you find them.*
>
> —Scott Stabile, self-help writer and speaker

Unlike Glenn, most of us can't move away and start over, so we need to be proactive in creating a lucky tribe where we are. This group will include people we already know but currently don't spend enough time with, as well as new people.

One way to identify your tribe members is by trusting your body's intelligence. You've already started this process in the address book/contacts exercise earlier in this chapter. Your body instantly knows who lifts you up—more quickly and clearly than your mind does. Learning to recognize the physiological markers that indicate you're with people who are good for you is simple. Pay attention to these internal guides:

1. **Your breath.**

    Look for the people around whom you breathe easier. That's a sure sign they're taking you to your essence, to who you truly are, rather than blocking you from deepening your self-love and understanding.

2. **Your eyes.**

    Look for people who make your eyes light up (and whose eyes light up when they see you). Like a true smile, this is an autonomic response—one that's instantaneous and can't be faked.

    It's said that the eyes are the windows to the soul. It makes sense that our eyes allow us to recognize the other members of our "soul community."

3. **Your solar plexus.**

    Be attentive to how you feel in your solar plexus—the spot below your heart and above your navel, in the center of your torso. We get a lot of information from the sensations we experience in that area: a sinking feeling in response to bad news, "butterflies" when we're excited, and the sense that our stomach is "tied in knots" when we're stressed. The solar plexus is the seat of our gut feelings. When you're around a member of your lucky tribe, you feel exhilarated there.

Attuning to these physical antennae is a great tool for determining which people you want to spend time with. The next step is understanding *how* to make the most of your time together.

Accelerating Your Conscious Luck Journey

> *Your tribe [will] get you through the tough days and give you something to laugh about on the ride.*
>
> —Nikki Rowe, author

The main emphasis of the sixth Conscious Luck Secret is surrounding yourself with positive people who want to see you grow and succeed, so if all you do is socialize—take walks, have meals, watch Netflix, or go to sports events or the theater—with people in that group, you're way ahead of the game. But if you want to strap on your Conscious Luck skates, we suggest taking additional actions, both alone and with others in your lucky tribe.

A powerful way to hang out with some of the luckiest, most influential people on the planet is through personal development audio programs, videos, and books. If you were to take fifteen to thirty minutes a day to soak up the wisdom available in libraries, in bookstores, and on the internet, you'd be amazed at the powerful positive impact this could have on your life. Anyone, anywhere, can take advantage of the support this universal lucky tribe offers.

If you're fortunate enough to have a flesh-and-blood lucky tribe in your vicinity, then we suggest finding a mentor, forming a mastermind/support group, choosing an accountability partner, or all three. (You will find resources in part 4 to help you accomplish this.) These are all great ways to connect with people who ask the right questions and who have the same vision. Your tribe members don't have to be highly successful. You're not "riding on the coattails" of lucky people. To change your luck, it's enough to be around people who think that's possible.

It's remarkable the extent people will go to further their growth. Gay once received an email from a woman who lived in a remote region of Pakistan. Once a month, she wrote, she would travel on foot from her village to a town twenty-five miles away in order to watch a film from the Spiritual Cinema Circle (a monthly video club Gay founded that offers its members inspiring, uplifting films). Someone in that town had a subscription and opened the viewing to others. This woman said she would set off in the morning, walk the twenty-five miles to arrive in time to watch the film in the evening, spend the night, and then walk back to her village the following day. She was grateful for this opportunity to see the films and for the expansion of her heart and mind that she experienced as a result.

Then there are those who face even more serious obstacles. Both of us have received letters from people in other countries asking us to send copies of our personal growth books—unavailable in their areas—so that they could form study groups and read and discuss the books together. In some countries, such as those in the Eastern bloc before the fall of the Iron Curtain and those with repressive religious regimes, these people were meeting secretly, risking their lives and freedom to better themselves and support others to do the same.

Take Advantage of the "Global Village" We Live In

It isn't where you come from; it's where you're going that counts.

—Ella Fitzgerald, singer

If you can't find people to meet with locally, you may have to go farther afield. Fortunately, with the internet, you can now do that without leaving your home. Canadian Sara Laamanen shared a story with us about what happened when, during a dark time in her life, she found a *virtual* lucky tribe:

SARA'S STORY

Surround yourself with those who only lift you higher.

—Oprah Winfrey

The only thing worse than being at an all-time low in your life is being there alone.

Two years before I found myself at that low point, I'd moved from my hometown in Ontario, Canada, to a tiny surf town on Vancouver Island in British Columbia (BC), so my ex-husband and I could raise our three kids, ages seven, ten, and thirteen, jointly. We'd both wanted to relocate and start over. I wasn't clear on my next steps and he was, so I agreed to go along with his choice, put the kids in school for a year, and take that time to figure out what I wanted to do with the rest of my life. My background was in real estate investing and property management, and I wanted to leave that all behind.

The one year had come and gone—twice—and here I was, in a town that still felt strange to me.

One of the main problems was that I just didn't fit in. I'm a city person: I love cultural events and going to fine restaurants, and I tend to dress up when I leave the house. I stuck out like a sore thumb in a place where flip-flops, shorts, and dreadlocks were the norm and there wasn't much to do besides surf.

But it wasn't just that. As I sat in my rented condo taking an inventory of my life, I realized there wasn't a single area that could be celebrated at that moment. I went down the list:

Work situation: dismal. I'd thought my stay on Vancouver Island would be temporary, and this had put me in a spiral of not committing to anything—I was doing a menial job, helping at the rental property where I lived.

Finances: stressful. I was living on my savings, with more money going out than coming in.

Love life: unfulfilling. I was dating without much success. Not long before the move, I had fallen passionately in love with someone very quickly, but the relationship hadn't worked out, and I was still nursing a broken heart.

Friends: too few. My regular support system was thousands of miles away, and while I'd made a few lovely new girlfriends locally, none were close enough to burden with my unhappiness.

Health: terrible. I was having autoimmune issues that I later learned were related to stress and lack of self-love.

Family of origin: a hot mess. My mother and I had been estranged for most of my adult life, and my father, whom I was very close to, had died before I left Ontario. I was fighting with my siblings over how to honor my father's final wishes, in terms of how the businesses he left behind should be run and how the assets should be divided. I was feeling a lot of tension about the situation.

The in-laws: crickets. When I was married, I'd had a lot of support from my ex-husband's family, but when we divorced, that dissolved. I was still mourning.

Relationship with my ex: not good. We were at loggerheads about everything. I'd tried to pack up the kids and leave one year after the move, but he'd taken me to mediation to keep the children in BC—and won. I felt trapped and resentful toward him.

Relationship with my children: fine! It was the only functional part of my life, though looking back, I see that even this was hampered by my own misery.

The inventory complete, I sighed heavily. On a scale of one to ten, I gave myself a "one"—a "two" on a good day. What was most discouraging was that I didn't see a way out and had no one to turn to for support.

For the next few weeks, I just kept putting one foot in front of the other.

Then it happened.

One day, going through my inbox, I opened an email from a bestselling author/transformational leader whose name I recognized. She was offering a yearlong personal mentoring and mastermind program called "Your Year of Miracles" for a group of eight women that seemed custom-tailored to my needs.

For a couple of years, I'd kept having the thought *I need a mentor—a woman in my life who can be my go-to person.* The prospect not only of having a mentor, but also of being in a group with seven other women, supporting each other "to live the life of our dreams," thrilled me to my core. An emphatic *Hell, yeah!* bubbled up inside me.

It was a big financial commitment, but I thought, *If I don't do this, I shudder to think what's next for me.* I filled out the application, had an interview, and to my delight was accepted into the program.

The very first moment we all met via Zoom, I knew I'd made the right decision. My mentor, her co-leader, and the seven other women were incredible—strong, beautiful, openhearted women, dedicated to growth and ready to help each other flourish. There was an instant feeling of transparency and authenticity among us.

We began our year together by setting intentions for ourselves—my intentions were to find the right place to live for me and my children, the right work, the right partner, and the right relationship with myself. We also committed to an intensive program of contact:

twice weekly calls or texts with an accountability partner, weekly calls with subgroups, monthly calls with my mentor, with her coleader who was also a mentor, with coaches, and with the whole group, as well as three in-person retreats.

My turnaround started immediately. We had our first group call in September, and based on the coaching from my mentors and with the encouragement of the group, I began looking for other places to live right away. My son and I decided to spend a weekend checking out Kelowna, BC, about four hundred miles inland from where we were on Vancouver Island. Within hours of arriving, I fell in love with the town and decided to move there.

The kids wanted to move with me, but as he'd done before, my ex said no. I told the kids, "Listen, I'm going to set up my life in Kelowna and make it attractive for you kids to come and for your dad to get on board. We'll see each other as often as we can."

It tore me apart to leave my children, but I saw no other option—I knew that moving was essential and that unless I did, nothing was going to get better.

At the end of October, just weeks into the program, I packed my car, drove to Kelowna, moved into a rental house, and started studying to get my Realtor's license in BC.

I can say without question that I would *never* have made that leap without the support of my group. When I was just inside my own head, I would think, *Oh, am I crazy?* But when I could bounce my ideas off this group of women—my "miracle sisters," as we called each other—who knew me and knew what my vision was for myself, I had much more confidence in my choices.

My accountability partner, Heather, and I bonded immediately. We touched in almost every day, either by text or by phone. There was a lot of listening and reflecting what we heard back to each other. When I felt Heather wasn't being honest with herself, I'd ask her clarifying questions. And she did the same for me. It made us face ourselves and our truth.

On top of that, I had lots of guidance from my mentor and from her coleader, as well as one-on-one sessions with the personal development experts brought in to work with our group. As homework, I read books, watched videos, and attended webinars on personal development. I was immersed in a culture of growth and co-creation.

My kids and I saw each other about once a month. Sometimes they came to me and sometimes I went to them. Even with that excruciating separation, my life was improving dramatically.

Fast-forward two years. Taking that same inventory today looks like this:

Work situation: hallelujah! I'm now a full-time hypnotherapist and transformational consultant. After a year in real estate, I decided to follow my true passion: helping others overcome obstacles. I trained in the modality of Rapid Transformational Therapy (RTT), and my work today is the most fulfilling I've ever done.

Finances: growing. I'm still building a clientele, but my finances are steadily improving. And I can tell you that being in the early stages of prospering at a career I love is a far cry from being financially stressed while working at an unfulfilling job.

Love life: marvelous. I'm with the best match I've ever been with. Not long after I arrived in Kelowna, I met a man through the real estate office where I worked. I was falling in love with my own life, and love seemed to miraculously find me, without much effort on my part.

Friends: many. I no longer feel isolated. I have a big network—partly from being with my new boyfriend, but more just because I'm happy, ready, and open. My joy seems to attract people to me.

Health: never better. With my stress level lowered significantly, my health began to mend almost immediately. Plus, through the mentoring program, I was introduced to a technique for eliminating self-limiting beliefs that had a remarkable healing effect.

My family of origin and in-laws: much improved. My in-laws and I have been rebuilding our relationships and visiting and chatting regularly. And my family of origin is mending and working our way to a new normal, with much more peace and respect between us.

Relationship with my ex: amazing. We're co-parenting really well. When he comes to visit, he even stays with me. And he and my boyfriend get along beautifully.

> Relationship with my children: they're here and thriving! After eight months of visiting monthly, the kids told their dad they wanted to move to Kelowna when school let out in June. He said, "I'm not moving."
>
> They told him that was okay and gave him all the reasons they still wanted to move. After mulling it over for a couple of months, he finally agreed they could come.
>
> This reversal by the children's father was the biggest miracle of all—aided in large part, I believe, by my decision, with guidance of the group, to change my perspective on my ex and think and speak only positively about him! Another breakthrough that would never have happened without my participation in this program.

Today on that scale of one to ten, I'm a "nine"—with flashes of "fourteen"! The phrase I say most often is "I love my life!"

✣

The mentoring group was the perfect thing at the perfect time. It brought me to where I am now by helping me rebuild my confidence and belief in myself. It also taught me the power of my own positive focus, magnified by the participation of others.

I now have a group of women I meet with regularly here in Kelowna. After that year of intense "sister connection," I'm drawn to women who are cheerleaders—who want to know what I'm doing and support me in any way they can. And vice versa. We know that when we reach out to each other, we're going to get that boost.

We can both vouch for the life-changing power of the right associations. For the last thirty years, Carol has met every other week with a women's group, sharing wins and intentions and offering support through rough patches and the upheavals that can come with change and growth. Over time, the members have come to live in different places, including New Zealand, so the meetings are held via phone. Coordinating time zones is complicated but doable. It's an appointment that Carol rarely misses.

Gay has also benefited from meeting with members of his lucky tribe. Early in his career, he and two other psychologists began getting together regularly. Though not a formal mastermind group, it turned out to be a place where the three could challenge each other's ideas and share down-in-the-trenches, real-life experiences. Gay says he probably learned more from those meetings than he did in his Ph.D. training: "For me, a lot of the value was in becoming more coachable instead of pretending I knew everything. I realized that if I became coachable in every moment, the world itself could become my coach. Today, after many years of growing my lucky tribe, I'm blessed with literally hundreds of people around the world who share the same positive outlook on life."

Who Is Fanning Your Flames?

Show me your friends and I'll show you your future.

—Mark Ambrose, author

The instruction to choose the people around you wisely is not a new idea. In the thirteenth century, the Persian poet and Sufi mystic Rumi wrote, "Set your life on fire. Seek those who fan your flames."

We're going to end this chapter with an eloquent if unorthodox commentary on Rumi's quote by actor and rapper Will Smith that we feel says it all about the people you elect to spend time with:

> Here's the Philly translation [of Rumi's quote]: Don't be hangin' with . . . jokers that don't help you shine. The prerequisite for spending time with any person is that they nourish and inspire you.
>
> There's been very few times in my life when I looked left or looked right and didn't find a person who believed and supported me. There's always been a person beside me fanning my flames.
>
> Look at your five last text messages—are those people feeding your flames or dousing your fire? . . . The people that you spend time with are going to make or break your dreams. Not everybody deserves to be around you. You gotta defend your light with your life.

✤

In the next chapter, we're going to explore how being true to yourself—on all levels—allows you to stay on the lucky side of the street.

7

THE SEVENTH SECRET

Learn to Be at the Right Place at the Right Time

The two most important requirements for major success are: first, being in the right place at the right time, and second, doing something about it.

—Attributed to Ray Kroc

If you ask people what it means to be lucky, they often answer, "Being in the right place at the right time." We agree that's a big part of luck, but how do you do that? Being in the perfect spot at the exact right moment seems completely outside our control. It's simply not possible for our limited human brains to consciously compute all the necessary variables.

The seventh Conscious Luck Secret offers a formula for dramatically increasing your ability to be at the right place at the right time: stay firmly rooted in your own center. Instead of relying on chance or looking for external direction to guide you to your lucky sweet spot, tune in to your own internal GPS.

This makes intuitive sense but is also rooted in science. Luck research shows that lucky people are far more likely than unlucky people to use inner guidance to make decisions about their relationships, career, and finances. Unlucky people, on the other hand, are prone to overthinking and waffling, afraid to make mistakes, and unwilling to trust themselves. Learning to function from your center is a crucial luck skill to practice. This includes moving your body at a rate that's in harmony with your core, listening to your intuition, and being true to your values, passions, and priorities.

Your Essence Pace

A crowded mind
Leaves no space
For a peaceful heart

—Christine Evangelou, "Head vs. Heart,"
from *Beating Hearts and Butterflies*

The vehicle for getting you to the right place at the right time is your body, but most of us walk around oblivious to what's happening inside us physically. We're distracted by what's going on around us or, more often, caught up in our thoughts, which are usually elsewhere—worrying about the future or regretting events in the past.

Operating at the speed of luck requires finding the stride that allows you to be present in *both* mind and body right where you are—in the moment happening *now.* You're not out in front of the moment or being dragged behind it.

We call that stride your "essence pace"—the speed at which you can move through space with a happy, sincere smile on your face. You can be moving quickly or slowly, but always with a sense of grounded ease. The key element is that you aren't stressed or anxious. When you move at your essence pace, you'll certainly enjoy yourself more, and in our experience, you're also more likely to arrive at the optimal spot at just the right time.

A story from Gay to illustrate:

> Some years ago, I was traveling for business and my plane landed late, making the connection time between flights very tight. The gates were far apart, and I had a long way to go in a short amount of time to make the connection. As I rushed through the airport, weaving impatiently around the crowds of people in my way, I caught my reflection in a polished surface on the concourse wall: head and torso thrust forward, a grim expression on my face. I consider rushing a sign of mental illness and there I was in the throes of it. So, I immediately slowed down and, taking a few deep breaths, found my center.
>
> Then I sped up again, but this time I stayed at my essence pace, conscious to maintain my centeredness. Now enjoying my walk through the airport, I rounded the corner of the concourse and approached my gate. There, at the podium, I saw a man berating the gate agent at the top of his lungs. "I will not be treated this way! Do you know who I am? I've got important business in L.A. You have to let me board this plane!"
>
> As I came up behind the man, I heard the gate agent say, "I'm so sorry, sir. I wish I could help, but the plane is full, and the doors are closed. We called your name three times. There's nothing more I can do."
>
> But the man ahead of me wasn't having any of it. He spun around, almost knocking me over, and stalked

away, still ranting. "I'll sue the airline for every penny they have. I'll own this airline! You'll regret this!"

Stepping up to the counter, I smiled ruefully at the gate agent. "One of those days, huh?"

The agent shook his head and blew out a breath. "You have no idea. . . ."

I was silent for a few seconds, letting that moment of connection be, then said, "Well, my initial flight was delayed, and it looks like I've missed this plane. What are my options?"

The agent had just begun tapping his keyboard to find the next flight when the door to the jet bridge opened and a flight attendant came bustling over to the counter to speak to him. I heard their whispered conversation: "Hey, there was a miscount. We've still got one seat left in first class."

I watched the gate agent's head turn quickly toward the angry man storming away up the concourse. The agent looked back at me, then glanced one more time at the man's rapidly retreating figure before again turning to me with a big smile and saying, "Well, sir, you're in luck!"

My essence pace, with a dash of common courtesy thrown in, had put me in the right place at the right time that day—and had even gotten me an upgrade!

Moving at the speed of luck requires letting go of whatever inside you is causing agitation in the situation. In Gay's case, he observed his anxiety about missing his flight and made the inner correction to come back to his own essence pace.

When you notice you're rushing, feeling stressed or anxious, or not present—either worrying about something that hasn't happened yet or ruminating about something that happened earlier—course-correct by stopping and taking a few deep breaths. As we learned in an earlier chapter, it turns out you're only three deep breaths away from feeling more centered.

Moving at your essence pace (or not) is a physical feeling, so from now on, as you move through your day, make a conscious effort to regularly check how you feel in your body, until traveling at your essence pace—and, by extension, the speed of luck—becomes a habit.

A good exercise for cultivating this awareness is to take a walk and, as you do, speed up and slow down, experimenting to find your essence pace in each moment. It could be different from minute to minute—you might be going uphill or down, or you might simply feel the inner urge to go more quickly or slowly. When you move at your essence pace, you can be going at any speed, but you always stay within your easy breath. Once you become familiar with how your essence pace feels in your body, it will be easy to stay in it and to realize when you need to make an adjustment to return to it.

Following Your Internal GPS

Don't ignore a hunch or silence your internal alarms just because you can't explain them. Lucky people act on these instincts.

—Margie Warrell, *Brave*

Another important gauge to monitor on your internal GPS is your intuition—that still, small voice inside that knows what to do and where to go and is indispensable for being at the right place at the right time.

Many successful people, including Albert Einstein, Jonas Salk, Warren Buffett, Oprah Winfrey, Nikola Tesla, and Winston Churchill, have valued and relied on their intuition. But this gift isn't restricted to the famous few. We believe that everyone has powerful natural intuition, but most of us overrule it.

Developing your intuition is an "uncovering" process. When you let go of relying exclusively on logic or intellect, you operate in a zone that seems magical and mystical but is actually much more predictable than that. All of us are factory equipped with incredible sensing tools, but we're not paying attention to the signals we receive.

For example, the Bushmen in the Kalahari Desert are renowned for being remarkable hunters. To outsiders, their ability to know exactly where to find their quarry appears uncanny, but their skill is more natural than supernatural: Bushmen's calf muscles sense the faintest trembling of the ground beneath them, alerting them to the movement of game animals, such as a buffalo herd, from up to nine miles away.

Consider also how little of the electromagnetic spectrum the human eye actually sees. We can perceive only in the range of 380 to 740 millimicrons—about 1/250,000th of that gigantic continuum. Beyond our limited perceptions, there are radio, infrared, ultraviolet, gamma, and X rays, plus a whole lot more we probably don't have any idea about—yet.

And of the sensory data that we do take in, our conscious

minds have learned to filter out 99.9 percent of it, because all that information isn't useful or necessary for immediate physical survival. **To access our intuition, we need to stop relying on what we're used to perceiving and tap into the subtle sensory discernment and inner knowing that's there at our disposal—even if we don't always understand it.**

Scientists have found that intuitions come from the right brain and other more primitive parts of the brain, as well as the gut, so those flashes of insight often don't make rational sense. Yet in repeated studies, the less analytical part of the brain knew the right answer long before the more logical part of the brain did.

Carol's husband, Larry, is a Vietnam veteran. Though he has strong left-brain talents—he's an engineer, builder, and businessman—he's also highly intuitive. Larry tells this story of the time in Vietnam when listening to his intuition made the ultimate difference in his luck:

> In 1973, I was stationed in Bien Hoa at the army base as a helicopter mechanic with the air cavalry. One afternoon, after working all day on the choppers, I decided to catch one heading to Saigon so I could grab a meal before guard duty that night. When I finished eating, I paid the bill and stood up to make my way to the helicopter going back to the base. Suddenly, I heard a voice inside my head say, *Sit down. Don't go!*
>
> Startled, I sat back down. But I was worried that if I didn't return on time, I'd get in trouble, so I stood up again. And again, I heard the words inside my head, *Sit down. Don't go!*

I'd had flashes of intuition before, but never so loud or clear. There was no mistaking the authority of this command. I knew another chopper was going back to the base in an hour, so I ordered another soft drink and hung out in the restaurant till it was time to leave to catch my flight. Once more, I stood up, my inner ear listening for the voice. Silence. *Okay,* I thought, *here I go!*

When I arrived back at the base, I found chaos—there had just been a rocket attack on the helicopters parked in the landing area. Everyone was shouting and running around, assessing the damage and making sure no one had been injured. As I approached my guard post on the perimeter, I saw that it was gone. All that was left was a huge crater in the exact spot where I would have been.

My fellow soldiers were searching the area for my body parts, because there was no way I could have survived that explosion. In their relief at seeing me alive, no one questioned why I hadn't been at my post. I couldn't deny my extraordinary luck, brought about 100 percent by listening to my intuition. To this day, I never question my hunches or inner commands, because so far, they've always served me.

✤

Heeding your hunches and gut feelings requires courage and commitment. And practice. But if you want to be in greater control of your own luck, it's enormously useful.

Improving your intuition, like learning to move more consistently at your essence pace, starts with a conscious effort to check in with yourself regularly, feeling for any inner yeses, warnings, or directives. Eventually, this inner connection will be automatic, and you'll be able to use your sixth sense as easily as you use your other five, to take in valuable information that helps you make the best decisions possible. And there's no question that good decisions lead to good luck.

Be True to Yourself

Find out who you are and do it on purpose.

—Dolly Parton, singer and actress

Imagine trying to scoop water with a sieve. Or captain a boat with a tattered sail. How successful will you be transferring the water or moving your boat forward? Not very. In the same way, trying to create more luck with holes in your "integrity bucket" simply won't work.

That's why the feeling of being in integrity with yourself is the final indicator to check on your internal GPS. And what exactly do we mean by integrity? Integrity is when who you are *inside* matches what you do and say *outside.*

Whatever your intentions, if your actions aren't aligned with your personal values and integrity, you're setting yourself up for a world of hurt. To maximize your good luck, always move in the direction of your personal true north.

How? A spiritual teacher of Carol's used to say, "Do what you *know* to be right." This is excellent advice for navigating everyday decisions, both large and small. For this Conscious Luck Secret, we would add two words: "Do what you *know* to be right—*for you*!" Maintaining personal integrity by honoring your unique values, passions, and priorities is our definition of being true to yourself.

Our friend Michele Roberts, a life and relationship coach, calls the act of honoring what's most important to you "making an integrity move." The most basic integrity move, she says, is committing to be your true self—or, conversely, no longer being willing to compromise yourself to fit someone else's idea of who or what you "should" be. When Michele made the integrity move to stop seeing herself through the lens of judgment—I'm too loud, too outspoken, too *much*—and accepted her New Jersey, Italian, passionate self, her luck changed for the better, especially in the arena of relationships. She became lucky in love, almost immediately drawing in her partner, Dean, who accepted and appreciated her just as she was. Michele says, "When I'm in integrity with myself, the universe responds—things seem to come my way, doors open."

Singer / songwriter and actress Cydney Davis has a beautiful story that shows perfectly how an integrity move, coupled with intuition, led to a remarkable and unexpected positive outcome in her career:

CYDNEY'S STORY

You already are all that you hope to be
Your beautiful truth rings clear

—Angela Predhomme, "Beautiful Truth"

From as far back as I can remember, I'd always had two loves—singing and kids. After college, I tried to honor both: I sang with a local band and became a middle school teacher in Toledo, Ohio, where I went to college. I made music and songs a big part of my classroom work with the kids. My students constantly told me: "Miss Davis, you could be a star!" "Your voice is so pretty." "You sing better than anyone on the radio!" "You should go to Hollywood!"

In 1982, I decided to listen to them. I quit the band, resigned from teaching, and moved to Los Angeles to pursue my dream of becoming a professional singer.

When I arrived in L.A., I got a job as a manager at a Target store to pay my bills and started to learn the music industry ropes—auditions, networking, and more networking! "Knowing someone who knew someone" seemed to be the magic ticket. But I didn't really know anyone like that.

In early 1983, a friend who worked for a security company snagged a backstage pass to the Grammys for me. I was so excited. That night, I dressed carefully in a white dress with rhinestones and matching white pumps.

At the Shrine Auditorium, I made my way to the stage entrance and stepped inside. There were a lot of people milling around and no one paid me much mind. The type of pass I had gave me only limited access to the backstage area, but I kept venturing deeper and deeper into the building. I made it all the way up to the stage without anyone stopping me. My friends all told me I favored Janet Jackson, so I think that helped.

The ceremony started. I stood in the wings, transfixed, watching the announcers in their glamorous outfits glide onto the stage to read the nominations and announce the winners. I couldn't get over my luck. There I was, no more than forty feet away from the biggest names in the industry: Lena Horne, Count Basie, Quincy Jones. Never in my wildest dreams had I ever imagined I'd be in the same room with them.

This was the night that Marvin Gaye, who had been nominated year after year, finally won—not just one, but two Grammys! After he accepted his awards, the audience gave him a thunderous standing ovation as he walked off the stage, directly to where I was standing! A crowd of people immediately surrounded him. There were reporters and photographers, as well as friends and family, hugging him, shaking his hand, and slapping his back. A line formed as more people waited to congratulate him on his well-deserved awards. I had always been a big fan of Marvin's and quickly took my place in the line, eager to meet him.

The line moved slowly, but I waited patiently. There were just two people in front of me when a little girl, perhaps nine years old, came up to me and said, "Hi! I really like your shoes! Can I try them on?"

I struggled with myself for a few seconds. As much as I loved children, I really wanted to meet Marvin Gaye. My idea was to give him my card and tell him how I'd always wanted to be one of his backup singers. This was my golden, once-in-a-lifetime opportunity!

But as I looked into the little girl's expectant eyes, I couldn't resist her. It just wasn't in me to shoo a child away. Besides, over the months I'd been away from teaching, I'd really missed interacting with my students. My love for children won.

"My name's Cydney, what's yours?" I said, stepping out of line and sliding one of my shoes off my foot.

"My name is Nona," she told me as she reached down to take off one of her shoes and grab mine.

I watched as she put the high heel on. It fit perfectly and her face lit up with a delighted grin. Then, abruptly, she turned and ran awkwardly in one flat shoe and one high heel through the crowd of people, straight to the great man himself. My eyebrows shot up as I saw her tug on his jacket, saying, "Hey, Daddy! Look at me!"

Marvin Gaye looked down and laughed. "Now where did you get that shoe?"

The little girl motioned to me and began dragging her father to where I was standing. "From my new friend. Her name is Cydney. Can she come with us?"

Stunned, I watched as Marvin Gaye reached out to shake my hand. "Hi, Cydney, I'm Marvin. Would you like to come to the after-party with us?"

Would I?? Of course, I said yes. And that was my introduction to Marvin Gaye's inner circle.

On that big night, I went to the party and hung out with Marvin and his family and friends. Marvin's kids and I just fell in love. Over the next couple of weeks, the kids kept in touch with me, inviting me to come over to the Ambassador Hotel where they were staying. I became a volunteer babysitter, watching the kids and at the same time observing all the musicians coming and going from Marvin's rooms as he created music.

I didn't recognize any of them but later learned that they were the top session musicians in the business. At one point, one of the guys sat down at the piano in the room where I happened to be, and I sang with him, but the only other person in the room with us was Marvin's secretary, Kitty.

I hadn't told either of Nona's parents that I was a singer. It seemed to me that everybody was always asking them for things. I wanted to be there for what they needed, which was helping with the children. I didn't want them to think I was using my friendship with the kids to get them to help me. But Kitty and some of the other staff knew I was trying to break into the business. I'd even given my demo tape to Marvin's valet, George, for him to give to Marvin. But Marvin hadn't said anything. Either he hadn't listened to it or he didn't think I was good enough. I was too shy to ask which it was, so I just let it go.

One night, a few weeks after the Grammy Awards ceremony, I left work at Target and started driving home. I found myself making turns that weren't on the route to my apartment. A voice—more a feeling—was giving me directions. I didn't understand what was going on but trusted that voice/feeling enough to listen. As I turned onto Wilshire Boulevard, I realized I was a block from the Ambassador Hotel. What in the world? The voice was clear: *Go to Marvin's office.*

I parked and thought, *What am I doing? I don't drop in on people! What am I going to say when I get there?* I decided I would ask about the children, as it had been a few days since I had seen them, and if they weren't there, I'd just leave.

I walked through the door and greeted Marvin's secretary. "Hey, Kitty, are the kids around?" I asked.

"No, they're not here," she said.

I shrugged and smiled. "Okay, well then, another time. . . ." And I turned to leave.

Kitty cocked her head. "I thought you were here for the auditions."

"A-a-auditions!?" I stammered.

"Yes, all these musicians you've seen coming and going? They're trying out for Marvin's next tour. And tonight is the last night for auditions to hire a new backup singer!"

At that moment, Marvin came out of one of the rooms and Kitty called him over. He gave me his biggest smile. "Hey, Cydney! How are you?"

Before I could reply, Kitty said, "Cydney's here to audition."

Marvin's eyes widened. "Can you sing, baby?" So much for George giving my demo tape to Marvin. . . .

"Yes, I can."

"Hold on." Marvin picked up the phone on Kitty's desk, punched in a number, and waited for the call to be picked up. Looking straight at me, but talking into the phone, he said, "Harvey, it's Marvin. I'm sending over a young lady. Her name is Cydney. I want you to audition her. If she really can sing"—here he winked at me—"if she can blend with the other singers, and if she has good pitch, I want you to hire her! She's good people."

I went to the audition, sang my heart out, and got that job. Singing with Marvin in cities around the country was a dream come true and just the beginning of a thirty-plus-year career in music, acting, songwriting, and more. After Marvin died, my time with him opened more doors for me. I went on to sing with Ray Charles, Barry White, Joe Cocker, Donna Summer, Stevie Wonder, Marilyn McCoo, and Billy Davis, Jr., to name a few. I wrote a song for Diana Ross and sang backup for her. Today, I'm still a working musician, teaching classes and acting in theater productions here in L.A.

I often marvel at the strange twists and perfect timing that got me to where I am today. Being true to my twin loves—children and singing—and trusting in myself has been a winning combination.

✤

We hope this chapter inspires you to follow your inner guidance more and more. A transformative alchemy, greater than the sum of its parts, happens when you embrace your body's natural pace, listen to your inner knowing, and are true to the promptings of your deepest self. When you stop *trying* to be at the right place at the right time and instead trust your inner GPS, you can be sure you'll end up in a lucky spot.

In the next chapter, we'll explore the final Conscious Luck Secret, which in and of itself, if practiced consistently and wholeheartedly, can create a life of outrageous good luck and joy.

8

THE EIGHTH SECRET

Practice Radical Gratitude and Appreciation

Gratitude is happiness doubled by wonder.

G. K. Chesterton, *A Short History of England*

Pssst! Here's a little secret about this Secret: If you had to choose just one Conscious Luck Secret to master, this is the one. For many people it's quite challenging, but if you can truly feel grateful *no matter what,* you've mastered Conscious Luck!

Please understand we're not talking about relentless positivity, whitewashing your experiences, or stuffing down your feelings—actions that fall under the umbrella of what is often called "spiritual bypass"—in the name of gratitude. In this chapter you'll learn how to stay centered emotionally and physically and, in authentic ways, find something to appreciate and be grateful for in every situation.

We'll also clarify the relationship between gratitude and appreciation, how both expand your "container" for luck, and why acting from a sense of entitlement has just the opposite effect.

Finally, we'll show you how to improve your luck by viewing the happenings in your life through a lens of innocence.

When you can reserve judgment about the lucky or unlucky nature of an event and adopt a more open, wait-and-see perspective about it, you'll often be spared a lot of unnecessary pain and upset.

Gratitude Basics

> *Gratitude unlocks the fullness of life. It turns what we have into enough, and more. It turns denial into acceptance, chaos to order, confusion to clarity. It can turn a meal into a feast, a house into a home, a stranger into a friend.*
>
> —Melody Beattie, author

Feeling lucky and feeling grateful are closely related. To understand their relationship, take a moment now to remember a time you felt lucky. If you're like most people, you felt elation, awe, upliftment, a sense of being taken care of, protected, or blessed, as well as a strong, overarching sense of gratitude for your good fortune. Similar to a Russian nesting doll, feeling lucky has many different qualities within it, but unpack the layers and you'll find gratitude at its center.

We can experience gratitude/feeling lucky as an exquisite sense of relief from worry or fear: the test results are negative, we find the valuable item we've lost, what sounds like a fender bender turns out to have caused no damage at all.

Or we can experience gratitude/feeling lucky as the exhilaration that comes with success: we get the promotion at work, our number is called at a drawing, we score an amazing deal on a purchase we've made. The central experience in all these is thankfulness.

Feeling grateful/lucky is the mirror image of feeling victimized. You feel grateful when you focus on what you *have* that you *want* (good health, financial stability, friends and family who love you) and what you *don't have* that you *don't want* (bad weather, car trouble, a trick knee). But switch that around and focus on what you *want* but *don't have* (no significant other, the lack of a fulfilling career, no time to putter in your garden or take a vacation) and what you *have* but *don't want* (an aging body, too many bills, a demanding boss), and you'll find yourself unhappy, complaining, and feeling like life's piñata.

The immediate antidote for victimhood is to switch your focus and lean into gratitude whenever you're in the throes of grumbling and stewing about your bad luck.

While writing this book, Carol had a conversation with a friend about the diametric relationship of gratitude and victimhood. Her friend, whom we'll call Aimée, at her request to protect her privacy, shared the following remarkable story about her experiences in that arena:

AIMÉE'S STORY

> *Gratitude, warm, sincere, intense, when it takes possession of the bosom, fills the soul to overflowing and scarce leaves room for any other sentiment or thought.*
>
> —John Quincy Adams

It was June 1985. I sat in the living room of our small rented apartment in Washington, D.C., crying in the dark. I didn't recognize my life. It had been a horrible day, a horrible month, a horrible year.

I grew up in Algiers, the pampered daughter of wealthy European parents. In our walled compound, servants had cleaned and cooked, and I had read, studied, and shopped. No one ever said no to me.

We moved to Israel when I was eighteen, and a year or so later, I fell madly in love with David, who was a little older than me, heart-stoppingly handsome, and a gifted woodworker. It wasn't long before we wanted to get married. As was the custom, David went to my father to ask for his blessing.

The two men sat in my father's study. After David explained his reason for coming, my father asked, "Are you sure you want to marry her?"

Seeing the surprise on David's face, my father lifted his hand in a conciliatory gesture and continued, "Don't get me wrong, my Aimée is the most wonderful girl in the world, and the apple of my eye, but she's not exactly wife material. She will spend all your money, and she can't even fry an egg."

David smiled at this and told my father none of that mattered. He could cook, and he would dedicate himself to taking care of me. "Although I can't give her the kind of privileged life she has with you, I love her, and she loves me."

Seeing David's sincerity and determination, and his obvious devotion for me, my father finally agreed.

When David told me he had my father's approval, I was jubilant. But David's face grew serious. After sitting me down, he made me promise that no matter what happened, I would never go to my parents for money.

"Yes, yes," I said, "of course," never dreaming how much this would affect us in the years ahead.

We married and soon had a daughter, Jacqueline. Our little family was very happy. In time, I even learned to cook! When Jacquie was three, David's closest friend invited him to come to America and be his partner in a custom furniture business: David would build the furniture and his friend would manage the money and the marketing. This was an exciting opportunity, and we gladly took it. We moved to Washington, D.C., and found a lovely house just outside the city. The business prospered and we loved our new community. Two years later, I got pregnant again. Life was good!

Then disaster struck. Our friend and business partner left the country and took all the company's money with him. We were devastated by his betrayal. Worse, we were left with nothing but a mortgage, the lease payments for the furniture workshop, and substantial debts for business materials.

I tried to convince David that we should ask my parents for help, but he was unmovable on this. We would figure it out, he said. End of discussion.

I had never experienced financial problems before. When I was growing up, money had been plentiful, and in our marriage, David and I had always been very responsible with our finances. We both believed in working hard and had never taken on any unnecessary debt, but it soon became clear that our only option was to declare bankruptcy. We both felt ashamed, but David was unwavering that we tell no one and simply do what we had to do. The bank took the house, we gave up the shop, and with the funds left in our personal account, we rented a clean but cramped apartment. David found temporary work that would tide us over till he could lease another shop and start again.

And then, more trouble. Not long after our move, Jacquie and I were coming home on the Beltway when our car started making an awful noise. I pulled over to the side of the road just as the engine sputtered to a stop. I turned the key again and again, but the car remained stubbornly silent. I leaned my forehead on the wheel, closed my eyes, and tried not to cry.

This was before everyone had cell phones, so I had two choices: walk for miles along the side of the busy highway with my child or wait for a policeman to come by and help us. I waited. A half hour later, an officer pulled up behind me and came to the driver's-side window. Taking in my barely contained tears and pregnant belly, and a wide-eyed Jacquie beside me, he kindly said he'd take us home; my husband could sort the towing and repair later.

Once home, feeling miserable, I lay down on the couch, keeping an eye on my daughter playing in the adjoining dining room. My mind kept spinning. *How would we pay for the car repairs? How could we pay rent on another shop? First and last months' rent and a security deposit were out of the question right now.* And, most painful of all, *How could we afford a new baby?*

Wanting to silence these thoughts, I pressed the power button on the TV remote. Nothing. I tried it again, but the screen remained blank. I pulled myself to my feet, lumbered over to the set, and pressed the "on" button. Still nothing.

Oh please, God, no. Not one more thing to repair. I flopped back down on the couch and stared at the dead TV. Overcome with self-pity, I let myself cry—silently, so as not to alarm Jacquie. Everything was falling apart. Maybe I had simply gone through my quota of luck and happiness, and it was my turn to suffer. I felt despair. What else would go wrong?

The tears continued to slip down my face as the room gradually darkened, matching my black mood. Finally, I asked Jacquie to please turn on the light.

Then, as the brightness spilled in from the dining room, I noticed a distinct shift inside myself. It was as if an inner light had come on.

What am I doing?? I asked myself.

I looked at my daughter's sweet, earnest face, lit with tenderness as she cooed to the doll she held in her arms. I saw the paintings and framed photos on the walls and the family treasures we'd brought from Africa and Israel on the dining room sideboard. Our little family was together. We were healthy. We had a roof over our heads.

Suddenly, like water breaking through a dam, everything that was good came pouring into my mind:

I had been able to pull out of traffic before the car died.
We had been able to wait inside the car, out of the sun.
The police officer had been so kind to drive us to our apartment.

We don't have money, but we're young and we can work.
My dear husband will be home soon. He will take me into
his arms and together we'll figure out what to do next.

I felt a wave of gratitude lift me up and I laughed—I was *so* lucky!

✤

That experience changed the direction of my mind and restored my courage. I was able to go forward with a new confidence.

We needed to rent a new shop, but with everything that had happened, our credit was shot. David was very grim about our prospects. Still, every day I looked at the paper and soon I saw an ad for a shop space that could work for us. I went to see the owners and told them we didn't have enough money for the required first and last months' rent and security deposit, but, I said, "we're hardworking and honest. We can pay the first month's rent only, but we will be with you forever."

The owner said, "I don't know why, but I believe you. I'll give you a chance."

I used the same approach for buying the equipment our business needed and for dealing with vendors and suppliers. Each time, I was honest yet upbeat, and it worked. David built and sustained the most successful custom furniture business in our area, right up until his retirement a few years ago. We had been our kind landlord's tenant for thirty years.

From that day on my couch to this one, whatever happens to me, I find the positive in it. It's a decision I make every morning when I wake and every night when I lay my head on the pillow to sleep. In truth, I make it in every moment. I believe this is how I've cultivated all the success that's come into my life since then, as well as the positive energy I sense all around me.

✣

Never underestimate the power of your focus—especially in times of distress. This can be challenging, because focusing on what we're grateful for and what's going well in our lives flies in the face of the inborn negativity bias present in all humans. This bias, which makes us register negative thoughts and events more deeply than positive ones, was necessary for avoiding life-threatening situations in more primitive times—helping us survive—but is outdated and counterproductive in today's world. It keeps us focused on what's wrong, rather than what's right.

Carol calls this the "small mark on the large canvas" experience. If there's a tiny spot on a large blank canvas, most people will focus on the spot, rather than the vast expanse of unmarred space surrounding it. You get ten compliments and one insult: which do you pay more attention to? In the same way, we spend a disproportionate amount of energy and time on the small things that are going wrong or need our attention, dramatically skewing our perception of the quality of our lives.

To enhance both our luck and our happiness, we need to learn to "slip the grip" of our survival wiring. The key is to be aware of the tendency to get caught in the negative *as it comes up* and then quickly course correct—without suppressing our emotions. (More on this later in the chapter.) If you can master the skill of intentionally switching your focus to authentically feeling grateful/lucky, this will truly change your luck—because *feeling* lucky is more important than *being* lucky.

Feeling Lucky Versus Being Lucky

Luck is believing you're lucky.

—Tennessee Williams, *A Streetcar Named Desire*

What's the difference between being lucky and feeling lucky? No, it's not a trick question—there is a difference. The answer is *feeling lucky* is a better measure of luck than whether you (or others) consider the events in your life to *be lucky.* We all know people we identify as lucky—born into wonderful families, financially secure, intelligent, talented, healthy—but if you ask them if they *feel* lucky, a large percentage of them will say no. Blinded by dissatisfaction about one or more aspects of their lives, they're oblivious to their gifts. Luck, it turns out, is subjective. Gay tells an excellent story about this:

> In 1980, I took my first trip to India. At that time, I was a backpacking hippie, but I still found the whole scene a bit overwhelming—the poverty, the crowds, the people sleeping in the streets, the beggars surrounding me, dozens of hands coming at me from all directions, clamoring for money. It took some time to get used to.

One day, I was sitting on the bank of a river, watching a group of about fifty kids on the opposite bank as they carried rocks up the hill behind them. None of these kids was more than about twelve years old. It was hard work performed under a hot sun. I asked an English-speaking passerby what was going on, and he told me a temple was being built on top of that hill and that the children had been hired to collect the rocks for the foundation. He said they were being paid one rupee (about a dime) a day for this job.

I sat, feeling outraged and sorrowful at what I considered their exploitation, until I noticed another group of about thirty kids sitting a little farther down the river, chins resting on their fists, faces glum, watching the other kids work. It turned out these were the kids who *hadn't* landed the job that day, and they were eyeing the rock carriers with envy at their good fortune.

As you can imagine, this experience dramatically reshaped my perspective on luck. Those kids working for a rupee a day were grateful for the job and felt lucky, though I hadn't considered them to be lucky in the least. I now saw my own luck in a new light—as strapped as I was cashwise, I was actually wealthy! I had more than enough money in my pocket to put the whole group to work for the next thirty days.

So, who's lucky? We say anyone who *feels* lucky. Fortunately, feeling lucky is entirely within your control. Next, we'll look at two ways to consciously cultivate feeling lucky: appreciation and the practice of Radical Gratitude.

Appreciation and Gratitude Are Not the Same

> *Appreciation is a wonderful thing: It makes what is excellent in others belong to us as well.*
>
> —Attributed to Voltaire

Many people use the terms "appreciation" and "gratitude" interchangeably, but although they're closely connected, they're not the same thing. We'll leave the lexicographers and philosophers to argue about the exact meanings; for our purposes, we offer the following definitions and distinctions:

> Gratitude is something you feel.
> Appreciation is something you do.
>
> Going deeper:
> Gratitude is feeling thankful for the people, places, and events in your life, including your health, your relationships, your possessions, your accomplishments—all the positive things that happen to you.
> Appreciation is active and a bit more complex. The word "appreciate" encompasses two types of actions—one internal, the other external.

INTERNAL APPRECIATION

When we stand in front of a Rembrandt or watch the play of moonlight on water, we "appreciate" the beauty we're perceiving. When we notice our spouse or a friend has gone out of their way to be helpful or kind, we "appreciate" their loving nature. When we savor a fabulous wine or a delicious meal, we "appreciate" the flavors we experience. These are internal acts of increased attention and awareness. To appreciate, you focus on an object deeply and perceive its qualities.

EXTERNAL APPRECIATION

Appreciation is also the external expression of that internal process. We "appreciate" someone when we thank them for something they did or for who they are. This can be done through verbal or written communication or a gift or a reciprocating act of kindness or aid.

If gratitude is something you struggle with, we suggest starting with the internal process of appreciating people, places, or objects, because the act of appreciating is a gateway to feeling grateful. And appreciation is something you can practice in any moment.

To deepen the appreciation process, pay close attention to the physical aspect of your experience:

Right now, look around and find something to appreciate—say, the color of the sky—then notice your body sensations as you're appreciating it. You'll likely feel a sense of expansion. The first thing appreciation does is open the body: your breath is fuller, and you perceive more—colors are brighter, and all your senses are more acute because you're giving attention to them.

Noticing your breath and your body sensations develops your appreciation receptors, heightening your ability to appreciate, which naturally expands your ability to experience gratitude. Over time, gratitude and, by extension, luck grow as a result of your repeated practice of appreciation.

But as they say in those cheesy infomercials: Wait, there's more! Appreciation has another luck-generating effect: expressing it makes you more attractive as a human being.

The Beauty of Expressing Appreciation

Appreciation can make a day, even change a life. Your willingness to put it all into words is all that is necessary.

—Attributed to Margaret Cousins,
American editor, journalist, and writer

It seems your mother was right: saying thank you and sending thank-you notes are important. Expressing appreciation develops deeper relationships, fosters collaboration, and helps you stand out. People remember people who appreciate them and are more likely to be helpful and supportive as a result. All these benefits contribute directly to experiencing more luck.

There's an important caveat here: this isn't a transactional move. Your appreciation must be sincere and appropriate—no Uriah Heeps, please. People can smell BS, and if you're sucking up to someone, it will have the exact opposite effect.

Appreciating a person, simply and naturally from your heart, by acknowledging his or her specific help or positive qualities, is as delightful an experience for the appreciator as it is for the one being appreciated. Expressing your delight with the world around you opens your own heart and makes you more radiant. People are drawn to the qualities of kindness and generosity.

Put this idea to the test: Think of the people you know who are gracious with their thanks and openhanded with their praise. Now, think of those who are stingy with their recognition of others and who are too self-involved to look outside themselves with wonder, awe, or admiration. When choosing a friend, a spouse, an employee, or an employer, which type of person will you select? And which group do you think will be luckier throughout their lives? It's a no-brainer. Cultivating gratitude and expressing it as appreciation is a surefire recipe for creating Conscious Luck.

That's why Stanford professor Tina Seelig, the luck expert you met in part 1, sits down after work each day and does an appreciation inventory. She looks at her appointment calendar, reviews the people she met with, and then sends each one a thank-you message. "It only takes a few minutes," she says, "but at the end of every day, I feel incredibly grateful and appreciative, and I promise you it has increased my luck." We recommend using Dr. Seelig's simple appreciation technique to improve your own luck as well.

Entitlement—the Hitch in Your Conscious Luck Giddyup

Entitlement is the opposite of enchantment.

—Guy Kawasaki, author, speaker, and entrepreneur

Gratitude has another marvelous benefit: when we feel truly grateful, we short-circuit any feelings of entitlement. Thinking you ought to have good luck just by virtue of who you are, where you were born, the sacrifices you've made—or whatever it is that gives you the idea luck ought to automatically come your way—is directly contrary to feeling grateful and a buzzkill for Conscious Luck.

Look at how nature works. If you're growing a crop, you go to the garden and water the seeds. You don't go out with a sense of entitlement and say, "Give me some zucchini and then maybe I'll water you." Gratitude is like watering the crops—it goes first, and the luck harvest comes after.

What's worse, according to our colleague Alison Armstrong, a relationship educator, when you get what you think you're entitled to, it's like getting a paycheck—there's no feeling of gratitude. This interrupts the Conscious Luck positive feedback loop: feeling grateful leads to more luck, which leads to more gratitude, and on and on. Without gratitude, you're left with a luck flat tire.

By now, it's clear that as Conscious Luck practitioners, we want to experience gratitude as often as we can. But is it possible to be grateful all the time? For most of us, the answer is no—unless we're willing to embrace the rest of the eighth Secret, which is to feel our feelings and practice a beautiful process of self-inquiry called Radical Gratitude.

To Feel or Not to Feel . . .

> *Spiritual bypass shields us from the truth, it disconnects us from our feelings, and helps us avoid the big picture. It is more about checking out than checking in.*
>
> —Ingrid Clayton, psychologist

Feeling lucky / grateful "no matter what" is a worthy goal, but it's important to take the right approach. Common gratitude advice like "Look on the bright side" and "Count your blessings," or anything that makes you feel you *should* feel grateful, can have the opposite effect or even be harmful. Trying to feel gratitude so you don't have to confront your own anger or sadness is a form of spiritual bypass—using spiritual principles to avoid negative emotions. It's like sticking a smiley-face Post-it note over a gaping wound. It may mask the problem, but it doesn't heal it.

If you're grieving the loss of a loved one and someone says to you, "Well, he [or she] is in a better place," it might relieve your pain temporarily, but like the pleasant flavor of a stick of spearmint gum, the relief wears off after a little while. This is because your mind has dismissed the need for sorrow (or fear or anger), but the emotion is still alive in the body—you feel your sadness and loss in your chest, your fear in your belly, and your anger in your jaws and clenched fists.

Too much spiritual bypass causes you to dissociate from your physical reality and end up like Mr. Duffy, a character in James Joyce's *Dubliners,* who "lived a short distance from his body." Being disembodied can numb your pain, but in the end it doesn't create a full, or lucky, life.

That's why it's important to feel all your feelings, and to feel them completely—all the way to the spiritual space of clarity and pure presence underlying them. Giving yourself permission to feel your uncomfortable feelings, rather than bypassing them, deepens your connection to what's real in yourself and the world. This is the true purpose of spirituality.

Feeling your feelings doesn't mean wallowing, indulging, or dramatizing your feelings. Those are on one end of the continuum, while stonewalling, stuffing, and using spiritual concepts to talk yourself out of how you feel are on the other. In the center is being sensitive and present to your feelings, however painful they may be. Then, and only then, do we suggest doing some gentle self-reflection by practicing Radical Gratitude.

Radical Gratitude

> *Can you be grateful that you're out of coffee? That your internet is down? That your team lost? If you have a brain and a bit of curiosity, yes you can.*
>
> —David Cain, from his blog, Raptitude.com

Radical Gratitude means being grateful for your challenges and struggles as well as your gifts. A tall order—especially when you're committed to going through, rather than around, what's difficult—but not impossible. And if you want to be luckier, it's an essential habit to establish.

Practicing Radical Gratitude is simple: the next time something bad happens, let yourself feel whatever comes up and then in the spirit of tremendously gentle inquiry, ask yourself, *Can I be grateful for this, too?* Remember, you're not trying to suppress or distract yourself from your pain or discomfort. There is no "should" or obligation to feel grateful—just a curiosity to see what answers surface.

When you invite yourself to consider the possibility that

there could be something to be grateful for, you'll observe how that shifts things and changes your perspective.

Writer, blogger, and meditation teacher David Cain, whose quote appears at the beginning of this section, gives us a glimpse of his experience with Radical Gratitude:

> I live in the city and make use of street parking every day. Most of the time I can't find a spot on the stretch near my building, and I have to drive past the building, around the corner, to the long side of the block. When that happens, I usually end up parking hundreds of yards away from my door with groceries to unload. Predictably I curse my bad luck, and often the people who parked where I wanted to.
>
> Just after I decided to try Radical Gratitude, this happened to me again. I was on the cusp of reenacting my normal sequence of overreaction—disappointment, maybe rage, then grumpy trudging—when I remembered the practice. Could I be grateful that I couldn't find a spot close to the building? Could what was happening be in any way a good thing?
>
> The thought immediately put me into a totally different position, one where I didn't assume I should feel any particular way about the longer distance to my apartment. Mostly I just enjoyed the walk, noticed a few of my neighbor's yard decorations, and felt glad that carrying grocery bags two blocks isn't particularly difficult for me. I'm lucky to be able to walk almost any distance without chronic pain or fatigue. It also struck

> me that my neighborhood is so close to downtown yet is peaceful and safe. I can walk through it at 4:00 A.M. with nothing to worry about.
>
> These are privileges that serve me every day, although I seldom actually enjoy them, because I'm so rarely aware of them. I arrived at my door feeling rather thrilled with my position in life, for exactly the way things were unfolding right at that moment.
>
> For me, Radical Gratitude is simply a way of challenging my initial feeling that a new development is wholly bad and that my moping and anger are justified—exploring instead what might also be good about it.
>
> Primarily, it does two things: 1) It forces me out of the hypersensitive autopilot I often operate under, which is based on the grievous misconception that events are isolated and are of two distinct types—good or bad—and that this goodness or badness is determined by how welcome it feels when it happens.
>
> And: 2) It puts me into a helpful problem-solving state that always ends in gratitude for something about what has just happened—the doors it opens, the things it teaches me, the future trouble it might spare me.

With enough practice, we can minimize our knee-jerk reaction of feeling stressed and distressed when something unwanted happens, freeing us to experiment with other responses and, in time, even create different realities. The ability to feel grateful/lucky at will is the essence of Conscious Luck!

However, there may be times when no matter what we do—switch our focus, appreciate someone or something, feel our feelings, or invite ourselves to consider what we could be grateful for—nothing works. We still feel unhappy and unlucky and that's just how it is.

When that happens, we suggest taking a few deep breaths—and a longer view. With the passing of time, what appears to be bad luck often leads straight to good luck. Look back at your own life: Was there an occasion when something unlucky paved the way for some wonderful new direction for you? Did losing your job free you up to find a better career? Was breaking up with someone, though devastating, the prelude to meeting your ideal partner? Did getting a diagnosis of diabetes, high blood pressure, or elevated cholesterol scare you into adopting healthier habits? Lemons often have a way of turning into lemonade.

And so, we come full circle. If you recall, the first Conscious Luck Secret is making a commitment to be lucky. Commitment means trying again and again and never giving up. Research has shown that the difference between lucky people and unlucky people is that lucky people are highly resilient, which comes in part from their ability to be grateful in the face of adversity.

When dealt a bad hand, unlucky people feel victimized, which we know is the opposite of gratitude. They usually feel so discouraged that they quit trying, shutting themselves off from future failures but also dashing their chances of future luck.

Lucky people, on the other hand, don't let setbacks make a dent in their commitment to being lucky. They look for the luck in every situation—win or lose—are grateful for it, and get right back on the horse. So, follow their example. A buoyant spirit keeps you taking action and allows you to stay open—to opportunities that pop up around you and to the contributions and support of others. This increases the likelihood of you being lucky a thousandfold!

This eighth and final Secret completes the Conscious Luck bridge we've been building together—the bridge that starts on one shore where you believe that luck is random, capricious, and mysterious and ends on the opposite shore where you understand that luck is, to a large degree, within your control.

Walk across the bridge with us. Use the Secrets we've shared to create a new and better life—one resplendent with dazzling luck in the areas of love, wealth, health, purpose, and contribution. We know it's possible, because we, and many others, have done it! All that's necessary is for you to take the steps yourself.

Practicing Is Perfect

> *We are made to persist. . . . That's how we find out who we are.*
>
> —Tobias Wolff, author

You now have an operational tool kit: the eight Conscious Luck Secrets—four that shift you at your core, changing the basic settings on your luck thermostat, and four daily practices that keep your good luck expanding day after day. They're all incredibly simple to do. The trick is *remembering* to practice them, especially when things first start to wobble in your Conscious Luck journey. If you remember to implement these tools sooner (rather than later, when the universe is busily whacking you over the head with something you're stubbornly resisting learning), you will have a much smoother ride.

To master these tools, we suggest you write the Secrets out in longhand, put them under your pillow when you sleep, tape them to your bathroom mirror, make a shrine to them, put them in your backpack on camping trips—do whatever it will take to make them a living reality in your everyday existence. They're *that* important.

In the next section, you'll find resources to support you in your Conscious Luck practice: information about an e-course to deepen your understanding of the Secrets, a forum for forming Conscious Luck support groups and finding accountability partners, and even an Emergency Luck Repair technique to employ if you get off track.

Use the resources, add to them, share them, and let them deepen your connection to others in the global Conscious Luck community. Once you feel launched on your own Conscious Luck path, consider becoming a Conscious Luck mentor to help others who share your desire to make the world a luckier place—one fortunate person at a time.

✤

Go now and be lucky. Practice what you've learned, and luck will accompany you everywhere, always.

We mean it.

PART FOUR

Keeping It Going

CONSCIOUS LUCK RESOURCES

In this section, you'll find ways to accelerate and stabilize the growth of Conscious Luck in your life.

1. Take Advanced Trainings to Deepen Your Luck-Change Experience

Visit our website, www.consciousluck.com, to find out about the Conscious Luck e-course as well as seminars, keynotes, coaching, and retreats.

2. Be a Part of the Conscious Luck Global Community

You're warmly invited to join the Conscious Luck Facebook group, where Conscious Luck events and discussions will be posted and where you can find local support groups and even arrange to have a Conscious Luck accountability partner. To join, go to bit.ly/consciousluck.

3. Emergency Luck Repair Technique

No matter how lucky you are, you can sometimes find yourself in a slump. (Remember, luck does have a small random component beyond our control!) So when you experience your luck going bad, here's a simple and effective technique to prevent the negative spiral from going further:

As soon as you become conscious that things are not going your way, stop what you're doing and immediately find one lucky thought—a thought that opens up possibility.

To illustrate, let's take an example from the gambling realm: imagine that you're at the poker table and you're on a losing streak. The biggest mistake you can make is to get into panic/fear mode and start chasing lost money. Chasing lost money is a sucker play from the get-go. That's because panic makes you stupid—it shuts down your brain's executive function so you can't make smart decisions. So, what do you do instead?

It may feel counterintuitive, but the best thing you can do is to step away from whatever you're doing, choose a lucky thought, and zero in on that. A lucky thought is one that puts you in a place of gratitude and appreciation for at least one thing in your life.

Here are a few examples of lucky thoughts:

Wow, I was really the luckiest person on earth to find my spouse!

I am so lucky to have such great friends.

I feel so fortunate to be healthy!

If you're really struggling, try this one: *A hundred million sperm started on the journey to fertilize the egg, and I'M the lucky ONE that made it there successfully! I definitely have something going for me!* It sounds silly, but for most people it's enough to disrupt the unlucky thought sequence in progress and switch the negative energy in a more positive direction.

Once you've found the thought, next you need to replace your panic-mode/fight-or-flight breathing with easy, flow breathing. Hold that lucky thought and take three long, slow, easy breaths. Or as many as it takes until you begin to feel some flow inside.

Once you've slowed your breathing and exited your panic state, you can go back to what you were doing with a renewed sense of gratitude and presence—which is an infinitely better state for making decisions about what to do next.

ACKNOWLEDGMENTS

Writing a book and getting it out into the world is both a solitary and group effort. We are so grateful for the many people whose help, participation, and cheerleading made this book possible.

A big thank-you:

To our agent, Bill Gladstone; our publisher, Joel Fotinos; his assistant, Gwen Hawkes; Katy Robitzski, Beatrice Jason, Alex Casement, Elizabeth Curione, Meryl Sussman Levavi, Sara Sgarlat, Nikolaas Eickelbeck, and the rest of the team at St. Martin's Essentials and St. Martin's Publishing Group.

To the many people who graciously shared their stories of luck and/or illustrations of one of the Conscious Luck Secrets:

Michele Roberts and Dean Yasuda
Glenn Agoncillo
Anand Amma
Crystal Dawn Rios
Krin Irvine
Alice Gannon-McKinley
Jason Su
Daniel Poneman
Paul Barnett
Jack Canfield
Steve Sisgold

Katie Anderson
David Cain
Chellie Campbell
Cydney Davis
Sara Laamanen
Alison Armstrong
David Byrd
Susie Moore

Though not all your stories could fit, we learned so much from your experiences and it made the book a better chronicle of how to change your luck.

To Lori Clelland and Cindy Buck, for their stellar editing work.

To Gail Motyka, for her generous help with technical questions.

And finally, to positive psychologist Dr. Richard Wiseman of the University of Hertfordshire, United Kingdom, and Dr. Tina Seelig of Stanford University, for their pioneering work in the field of luck research.

GAY'S ACKNOWLEDGMENTS

I am grateful to many people who helped with the ideas in the book, the writing itself, and getting it into your hands. First, my deep gratitude to Carol, whose clear mind and stellar writing talents made *Conscious Luck* a dream to work on. A belated bow of thanks to Jack Canfield, for introducing me to Carol many years ago. Big thanks to Bill Gladstone, agent, friend, and fellow golfer, for connecting us up with the legendary Joel Fotinos of St. Martin's Essentials, Gwen Hawkes, and the team.

I am grateful to Norma Hendricks, my mother, especially for teaching me about the discipline of writing. Mom wrote a daily newspaper column throughout my growing-up years. She had to get the column in by seven o'clock each night, and she never missed a deadline, even one time when her car wouldn't start and she had to pedal off to the office on a rickety bike. I also want to salute the memory of my freshman English teacher at Rollins College, the late Dr. Stephen Sanderlin. He taught English composition with a passionate zeal, as if he were personally defending Western civilization from the advancing barbarian hordes. From him I learned how to write a topic sentence, craft a paragraph, and choose unusual verbs to add verve and sensory texture to my writing.

My eternal gratitude to my wife, Dr. Kathlyn Hendricks, for forty years of love and great times. I'm very blessed to have a mate who is both my muse and my first listener. One of our sacred traditions is that I read aloud to her everything I write each day. Her generous listening and helpful suggestions make writing a daily joy.

CAROL'S ACKNOWLEDGMENTS

My heartfelt thanks go to so many people, starting with my coauthor, Gay Hendricks. Gay, you are a man among men! I love your wisdom, your humor, your generosity, and your superpower of making people feel brilliant in your presence. Thank you for trusting me to collaborate on what began as your vision and has become our shared offering to the world.

I am grateful beyond measure for the precious gift of sitting with you regularly to discuss the secrets of luck, love, and life.

Thank you also to Katie Hendricks, for sharing your treasure of a husband and partner with me while we wrote this book and for contributing your views on luck, appreciation, and gratitude—as well as your Conscious Luck story of overcoming fear through badassery.

Gratitude in great amounts goes to:

My walking buddy and editor extraordinaire, Lori Clelland. Thank you, for your thoughtful (sometimes snarky) editing, your picky corrections, and your cheerleading and positive feedback. You are a delight on so many levels.

My longtime friend, collaborator, and editor, Cindy Buck. I'm so grateful to you for your time and attention to Aimée's story. As always, you improved it and made me appear a better writer than I am!

My dear friend and go-to grammar/punctuation expert, Jennifer Hawthorne. Thank you for caring as much as I do!!

My sometime coauthor and always best friend, Marci Shimoff. Thank you, for your enthusiasm for this topic in particular and for my writing in general. Thank you, also, for taking time from your crazy-busy schedule to read the manuscript and give your incredibly valuable feedback. Your encouragement and friendship mean the world to me. I love you whole tons.

My women's group, Karen Joost and Toni D'Orr. Though our lives are so different—life stages, outlooks, and even continents—you will always be my safe harbor. Thank you, for your consistent support and interest in my ventures and adventures!

My soul-sistah, Debra Poneman. Deb Sue! Thanks, for being such a bright light on this planet and especially in my world. I admire your dedication to bodhisattva-ness with a grounding in fun. You have a talent for making your friends feel loved.

My soul-nephew, Daniel Poneman. You are a true mensch. Even as a little boy, you inspired me with your huge heart and gift for helping others. Thanks for being a great role model for Conscious Luck. I know you'll do well, because you're always doing good.

My mentor and friend, Jack Canfield. Through the years you've charmed and empowered me with your accepting presence, balanced mind and heart, and gentle humor. Thank you, for allowing us to use your story in this book and for all the ways your presence in my life has enriched it.

To my sister-in-law, Patrice Quinlan. Thank you, for your sweet support and love—and for connecting me to Cydney, who contributed so much to this book.

To the one and only Elizabeth Reynolds, who is smart, beautiful, and funny, and who not only lets me be silly—but joins in. I'm so grateful for our time together and your stalwart belief in me.

To my mermaid in chief, the darling Allison Stillman. Thank you, for years of loving sisterhood—going on walks, eating amazing meals, having looooong talks, pursuing side gigs, getting and losing our fur-kids, and inspiring me with your ability to create beauty wherever you go. You, my dear, rock.

To my friend Anne Kerry Ford, for your love of beauty and truth and your willingness to talk about anything and everything: luck, gratitude, the nature of reality, and, of course, cake-pops!

To the soul of kindness, Karen Palm. Thank you, for your easygoing nature, your enormous talent for listening, and, most especially, your consistent and enthusiastic cheerleading. I don't know if I could have made it through the book-writing process without you.

To D. C. McGuire, my sweet friend, your gentle, loving spirit is always balm to my soul.

To my Ojai women friends, Carol Cilliers, Diana Feinberg, Debbie Petcove, Sharon Olisky, and Susan Bruce. I met each of you while walking, and now you are my favorite walking buddies. Thank you, for getting me out of my office and into the fresh air on a regular basis.

To my spiritual teacher, Sri Sri Ravi Shankar. Your wisdom, spiritual techniques, and guidance are at the heart of my days. I can never thank you enough.

To my family: my siblings and their spouses and children, for their general beneficence and well-wishes.

To Buddy Boy, the smartest, funniest, handsomest dog ever.

To my amazing husband, Larry Kline, who is talented, kind, gorgeous, resourceful, and my rock. Every day you make me laugh and feel like the luckiest woman in the world. I hit the jackpot when I married you.

ABOUT THE AUTHORS

Gay Hendricks has been a leader in the fields of relationship transformation and body-mind therapies for more than forty-five years. After earning his Ph.D. in counseling psychology from Stanford University, Gay served as professor of counseling psychology at the University of Colorado for twenty-one years, then went on to found the Hendricks Institute, which offers seminars in North America, Asia, and Europe. Throughout his career, he has coached more than eight hundred executives, including the top management at firms such as Dell, Hewlett-Packard, Motorola, and KLM.

Dr. Hendricks has written more than forty books, including bestsellers such as *Five Wishes, The Big Leap,* and *Conscious Loving* (coauthored with his mate for more than forty years, Dr. Kathlyn Hendricks), the last two used as primary texts in universities around the world. In 2003, Gay cofounded the Spiritual Cinema Circle, which distributes inspirational movies and conscious entertainment to subscribers in seventy-plus countries.

Gay has offered seminars worldwide and appeared on more than five hundred radio and television shows, including *The Oprah Winfrey Show,* CNN, CNBC, *48 Hours,* and others. In recent years his passion has been writing mystery novels.

Carol Kline has been an author, editor, and ghostwriter for more than twenty-five years. During that time, she's coauthored fourteen books with some of the world's top transformational leaders—including six books in the bestselling Chicken Soup for the Soul series with Jack Canfield and Mark Victor Hansen; *Happy for No Reason* and *Love for No Reason* with Marci Shimoff; *No Matter What!* with Lisa Nichols; and *You've Got to Read This Book!* with Jack Canfield and Gay Hendricks. Five of those books went on to become *New York Times* bestsellers.

Inspired by her experience writing *Chicken Soup for the Pet Lover's Soul* in 1997, Carol became deeply involved in animal rescue work and helped run and build an animal shelter called Noah's Ark Animal Foundation in Fairfield, Iowa. She now lives in Ojai, California, with her husband and is at work on several writing, business, and service projects.

CONTRIBUTOR BIOS

Glenn Agoncillo (chapter 6) is an entrepreneur, genius catalyst, and cultivator of magic. Glenn resides in Long Beach, California, with his husband, Michael Tawney, and their dog, Fred. www.glennagoncillo.com

Katie Anderson (chapter 4) is the founder and CEO of Save Water Co. Her entrepreneurial spirit and passion for addressing the world's water issues have attracted attention, garnering her recognition as one of *Forbes* magazine's "30 Under 30" and winning laureate of North America for the Cartier Women's Initiative Award. In five years, her company has implemented conservation measures on more than sixty thousand apartment units, saving more than 2.2 billion gallons of water, deferring over one thousand tons from entering the landfills, and highlighting the possibility of for-profit companies doing sustainable social impact ventures. www.savewaterco.com

Alison Armstrong (chapter 8) is an author and relationship educator who has been designing and leading transformational programs for adults for almost twenty-five years. Find out more about her and her live seminars for men and women at www.understandmen.com.

David Cain (chapter 8) is a writer and entrepreneur based in Winnipeg, Canada. He writes about well-being and the human experience at www.raptitude.com.

Chellie Campbell (chapter 5) treats money disorders—spending bulimia and income anorexia. She is the creator of the Financial Stress Reduction Workshop and the bestselling books *The Wealthy Spirit, Zero to Zillionaire,* and *From Worry to Wealthy.* www.chellie.com

Jack Canfield (chapter 4) is a coauthor of the *New York Times* bestselling Chicken Soup for the Soul series and *The Success Principles: How to Get from Where You Are to Where You Want to Be* and a featured teacher in the book and the movie *The Secret.* www.JackCanfield.com

Cydney Wayne Davis (chapter 7) is a professional singer, songwriter, actor, vocal coach, and playwright who has toured and recorded with artists such as Marvin Gaye, Ray Charles, Joe Cocker, Marilyn McCoo and Billy Davis, Jr., Stevie Wonder, and Diana Ross. She is the recipient of the 2013 NAACP Theatre Award for Best Supporting Actress, and her film credits include *Basketball Girlfriend* and *Chocolate City* as the feisty church lady, "Sister Beatrice." www.cydneywaynedavis.weebly.com

Sara Laamanen (chapter 6) is an expert in human transformation and practices as a clinical hypnotherapist and Advanced RTT practitioner, helping her clients achieve emotional freedom rapidly by dissolving conditions such as anxiety and chronic anger. She is also passionate about working with teens and sees their emotional freedom as a massive change agent for the world and humanity. www.saralaamanen.com

Susie Moore (chapter 5) is a life coach, advice columnist, and author of two books, *What If It* Does *Work Out?* and *Stop Checking Your Likes*. Her work has been featured on the *Today* show, *Oprah*, *Business Insider*, *The Huffington Post*, *Forbes*, *Time Inc*, and *Marie Claire* and she's the resident life coach columnist for the health and wellness site, Greatist. www.susie-moore.com

Daniel Poneman (chapter 4) is a twenty-seven-year-old sports agent from Chicago, representing players in the NBA, NFL, and international leagues, and a cofounder of Beyond Athlete Management. Additionally, Daniel is chairman of the Shot in the Dark Foundation, a 501(c)(3) dedicated to helping young people get free college educations through basketball, and producer of various sports documentaries, including *Shot in the Dark*, which premiered on Fox in February 2018. www.beyond.am

Michele Roberts (chapter 7) dances in the field of infinite possibility and sparks discovery and transformation. Michele is a Big Leap Coach and graduate of the Hendricks Leadership and Transformation Program and can be found at www.micheleanddean.com.

Steve Sisgold (chapter 5) is a speaker, trainer, executive coach, blogger, and author of the bestselling books *What's Your Body Telling You?* and *Whole Body Intelligence*. He has taught thousands of people his Whole Body Intelligence program to lower stress, boost performance, change limiting beliefs, and create more authentic relationships. www.wholebodyintelligence.com

THE 8 SECRETS TO INTENTIONALLY CHANGE YOUR FORTUNE

1. Commit to Be a VLP—Very Lucky Person

2. Release Your Personal Barriers to Good Fortune

3. Transform Shame into a Magnet for Abundance

4. Have Luck-Worthy Goals

5. Take Bold Action Consistently

6. Find Your Lucky Tribe

7. Learn to Be at the Right Place at the Right Time

8. Practice Radical Gratitude and Appreciation